The Pitcher *and the* Dictator

The Pitcher *and the* Dictator

Satchel Paige's Unlikely Season in the Dominican Republic

AVERELL "ACE" SMITH

UNIVERSITY OF NEBRASKA PRESS | LINCOLN & LONDON

Library of Congress Cataloging-in-Publication Data
Names: Smith, Averell, author.
Title: The pitcher and the dictator: Satchel Paige's unlikely
season in the Dominican Republic / Averell "Ace" Smith.
Description: Lincoln: University of Nebraska Press, 2018. |
Includes bibliographical references and index. |
Identifiers: LCCN 2017036451 (print)
LCCN 2017058331 (ebook)
ISBN 9781496206695 (epub)
ISBN 9781496206701 (mobi)
ISBN 9781496206718 (pdf)
ISBN 9781496205490 (hardback: alk. paper)
Subjects: LCSH: Paige, Satchel, 1906–1982. | Trujillo Molina,
Rafael Leónidas, 1891–1961. | Baseball—Dominican
Republic—History. | Dragones de Ciudad Trujillo (Base-
ball team)—History. | Dominican Republic—History—
1930–1961. | Pitchers (Baseball)—United States—Biography.
| African American baseball players—Biography. |
BISAC: SPORTS & RECREATION / Baseball / History. |
SOCIAL SCIENCE / Ethnic Studies / African American
Studies. | HISTORY / Latin America / Central America.
Classification: LCC GV865.P3 (ebook) | LCC GV865.P3 S64
2018 (print) | DDC 796.357092 [B]—dc23
LC record available at https://lccn.loc.gov/2017036451

Set in Sabon Next by Mikala R Kolander.

For Lili Rachel Smith

If you are sad think of her smile.

If you are struggling think of her determination.

If you walk through the world fighting for
human rights and equality, glance down at your
side for she will be there.

In Memoriam

En un mortífero ataque,	In a deadly attack,
Los Dragones con coraje,	The Dragons with courage,
Le quitaron el plumaje	Took the plumage
A las Águilas del Yaqué.	From the Eagles of the Yaque.
Cuando a Matlock a lanzar	When Matlock threw
Lo pusieron de tapón,	They put in the stopper,
No encontró tirabuzón	And could not find a corkscrew
Que lo pudiera sacar.	Able to extract it.
De la situación ya dueño,	As master of the situation,
Un magnífico collar	A magnificent necklace
De Ceros pudo colgar	Of Zeros he hung
Al equipo Cibaeño	On the team Cibaeño
Cargaron con la derrota,	They loaded with defeat,
Pues al muy notable Dihigo	The most remarkable Dihigo
Tan habiendo ya vencido	So having already defeated
Al equipo Cibaeño	The team Cibaeño
Se lanzó con gran empeño	I am thrown with great effort
A la Ciudad de la caña	To the City of Cane
Donde con crueldad y saña	Where with cruelty and fierceness
De Macorís se hizo dueño.	Of Macorís they became master.

Allí fue que Cocaína	There was that Cocaína
Explotó como un cañón	I blow up like a canon
Y que Paige sin compasión	And Paige without compassion
A la bola unto morfina.	To the ball unto morphine.
No valió la lloviznita	It did not cost the drizzle
Que dañar el juego quiso,	That the game wanted to damage,
Ni el tablazo de Mellizo;	No even in a blaze of Mellizo;
Tampoco Luis NAVAJITA.	Nor Luis NAVAJITA.
Y fue tan grande el plumaje	And so great was the plumage
Que a las Águilas quitó …	That he took from the Eagles …
Y fue tanta la caña	And it was so much cane
Que en la Sultana Molió …	That in the Sultana Molio …
Que con esta situación,	That in this situation,
Este animal sin entraña	This animal without heart
Al que llamamos Dragón.	Whom we call Dragon.
Seguirá moliendo cañas	He will keep on grinding canes
Reclinado en su sillón.	While reclining in his chair.
Del cielo cayó una estrella,	From the sky a star fell,
Dios la lleve a buen lugar …	I took it to a good place …
Con esta frase tan bella	With this beautiful phrase
Acabo de terminar.	I have now ended.

—G.A.S.

Poem published in *Listín Diario*, June 29, 1937,
near the end of the championship series

CONTENTS

Recovery of a Lost History

I fell in love with baseball when I was twelve years old. That year I bought the 1956 edition of *The Official Encyclopedia of Baseball* for ten cents at my school's annual rummage sale. How I pored over that magical book at every opportunity—it had stats for every player who ever played in the Majors, records by season, best lifetime marks, a chapter chronicling every World Series, and even diagrams with measurements of each ballpark (I was consumed by the jagged design of Polo Grounds with its 258-foot right-field porch and what appeared to be a missing tooth in center field). The section that mystified me most was the less-than-one-page "Negro Players" sandwiched between two features, "One-Day Major Leaguers" and "Spitball Pitchers." The book drily notes that "only one of the fabled figures of this lost chapter in baseball history managed to benefit through modern emancipation: Leroy (Satchel) Paige, though well past 40 at the time, joined the Indians and helped pitch them to the pennant in 1948."[1]

With perseverance a group of passionate souls pried loose the subject of the "Negro Players" section from its place between "One-Day Major Leaguers" and "Spitball Pitchers." We owe a debt of gratitude to the pioneering works of A. S. "Doc" Young, John Holway, William Brashler, Mark Ribowsky, James Riley, and Donn Rogosin. Peter Bjarkman and Roberto González Echevarria have shone a much-needed light on Caribbean baseball of that era. And of course the Dominican Republic has the magnificent trio of historians, Cuqui Cordova, Orlando Inoa, and Héctor Cruz.

I am especially grateful for the kind help I received from Emmanuel Rodrigues at the Dominican National Archives and Adriano Tejada, who has been the publisher of many important histories of Dominican baseball. My sincere thanks go to everyone at the University of Nebraska Press who helped bring this project to fruition, especially Rob Taylor, whose early enthusiasm for the book encouraged me along the way, and Joeth Zucco, the project editor who skillfully oversaw the book's transition from manuscript to published volume. I also wish to thank my wonderful freelance copyeditor, Barbara Wojhoski.

Perhaps the best writer of them all was Satchel Paige. Paige wrote the entertaining short book *Pitchin' Man* when he broke into the Majors with the Cleveland Indians in 1948. After retiring he took time to write his autobiography, *Maybe I'll Pitch Forever*, which was published in 1962. Because it was written by a baseball player, it will never be viewed as a serious literary work, yet I believe it is the *Huckleberry Finn* of the twentieth century.

I can only hope that my little book opens more eyes to the mighty and heroic struggles of African Americans in the United States.

The Pitcher *and the* Dictator

1

Trujillo City

If I didn't show them now, they'd never believe
I was one of the greatest of all times.

—SATCHEL PAIGE before pitching in his
Major League debut at age forty-two

Satchel thought it was all so odd. He expected to play on the tight schedule he had grown accustomed to—on the bus, off the bus, lousy hotel, worse food, ball game, next town same thing. It had gotten to the point where he felt like a traveling salesman who hardly knew what town he was in on any particular day.

This was different. He found himself on an island where the weather was warm, the tempo relaxed. Where the games were in just three cities. Even better, they played only on weekends. A nice club in the capital city was his headquarters. And best of all, despite the color of his skin, Satchel and his friends had been able to eat, drink, carouse, and sleep anywhere they wanted—things he couldn't do freely in 1937 in the land of the free, home of the brave.

After a few days Satchel felt the tempo of Ciudad Trujillo (Trujillo City) in the Dominican Republic in his bones. People filled the streets promptly at 8:00 a.m. When noon arrived, the streets were flooded with businessmen in white suits wearing banded white hats. They came pouring out of stores and offices to head home for a lunch of soup, chicken or pork and depending on the day or mood, potatoes, beans, rice, plantains, melon, pineapple, tomato, and heart of palm salad, with pudding and coffee to finish.[1] An hour-long siesta followed. At 1:45 sharp, to wake the napping populace, a pair of shrill ochre-colored, snail-shaped sirens, mounted on a tall white bell tower, were blown.[2] Oddest of all, when the newspapers had a big story, the same sirens announced the scoop to the citizenry.[3]

As he walked through the city, Satchel shook his head and blinked at what he didn't see: beggars, trash, vagrants, or bare-footers. Streets were mostly paved. They were immaculately clean. Calle El Conde, the artery of the tony shopping district, was crowded with jewelers, clothiers, restaurants, and cafés. The *calle* clattered with motorcars and every variety of horse-drawn contraption. It seemed as if all the buggies and carriages that had disappeared from the streets of the United States had been transported whole cloth to the streets of Ciudad Trujillo. Satchel would hear their musical warning bells and turn to see the glimmer from the brass trimmings of hansoms, landaulets, cabriolets, victorias, surreys, herdics, and fiacres.[4]

He found, without a doubt, that the most beautiful spot in the city was the palm-lined esplanade, which followed the contours of the Caribbean. Called by locals El Malecón (the Breakwater), it was skirted by Avenida George Washington, which was spotted with benches and meticulously manicured parks filled with well-dressed children. The *avenida* led to a freshly installed white marble obelisk, which was a one-quarter-size replica of the Washington Monument. He later learned that even though it stood on Avenida Washington, the obelisk wasn't dedicated to George Washington.

2

Time to Get a Job

The hot days in the Dominican Republic, cooled by an ocean breeze, felt the same to Satchel as when he had walked along the seashore of the Gulf Coast in Mobile Alabama, as a child. He still remembered that day his mother had looked him in the eye and told him it was time to get a job, time to help support his family. He was six. But there wasn't much choice; the family had to put food on the table, and that meant everybody had to contribute. After all his nine-year-old brother already had a steady job. At first the younger boy began by collecting bottles from trashcans and bathrooms to sell to bootleggers. When he turned seven, his mother told him that "bottle selling wasn't enough." It was simple; she said he needed to get a "job somewhere to help out more." It made the child feel like he "was fifty or sixty years old."[1]

His mother told him he could make more money carrying bags at the train station. So for a dime each, the little boy began carrying bags for travelers arriving in the segregated city of Mobile, Alabama, in 1915. This clever child wanted to improve his income, and he got to thinking: "One satchel, one dime. Two satchels, two dimes. Three satchels, three . . . the more satchels, the more dimes."[2] So he began stringing the satchels to himself and onto a pole. He knew his invention "wasn't a smart-looking thing," but on a good trip he "could string up sixteen satchels, put one under each arm and two in [his] hands" for a two-dollar haul.[3] The other children laughed at the sight of this small child walking around town loaded down with satchels

3

strung to his odd invention. "You look like a walking satchel tree," they teased.[4]

So he got the name "Satchel."[5]

Satch.

    Satchel.

        Satchel Paige.

He was born Leroy Robert Page in Mobile, Alabama, in 1906.[6] At first Satchel's family name was the common "Page," but his father added an extra "i" to make the name sound more "high tone." Satchel's mother was a washerwoman as well as the undisputed boss of the house. The eleven Paige children and the family goat lived in a four-room "shotgun" house. Often they relied on vegetables from a backyard garden or fish caught in the nearby bay.

Satchel grew up in a time of bitter racial oppression. Reconstruction had ended in Alabama in 1874 when a group of ex-Confederates seized control of state government and began passing a series of Jim Crow laws, transforming Alabama into an apartheid state. By the turn of the nineteenth century, lynchings had become commonplace in Mobile. Between Satchel's birth and his fourth birthday, five Mobile blacks died at the hands of white lynch mobs. Violent mobs became so emboldened that they staged one of these lynchings across the street from the city's oldest church.[7]

One summer day twelve-year-old Satchel was arrested for shoplifting a handful of brass rings and sentenced to live out his adolescence at the Alabama Reform School for Juvenile Negro Law-Breakers in Mount Meigs.[8] When Satchel arrived back in Mobile in December 1923, he was a young man determined to become a baseball star.

Two years after returning home, Satchel signed his first professional contract with Mobile native Alex Herman of the Chattanooga White Sox, in April 1926.[9] He pitched opening day and was an immediate sensation.

Eleven years later, on a warm July Sunday, Satchel shook his head in disbelief as he found himself walking along the streets of Ciudad Trujillo. The city was vibrating to the pulse of *un gran festival*. By 6:00 a.m. thousands had tuned their radios to the powerful station with the call letters HIX to hear the drawing of the lottery numbers. Two violinists played to hundreds gathered at the central lottery offices, standing, watching as the colossal wire globe was spun on its axis. Like a roulette wheel, when it slowed, it tossed out a ball, and the numbered ball fell into a wire basket. "Numero siete," intoned the bald man with thick glasses. When the numbers lay in the basket, a smaller wire globe was spun. It slowed until it spit out the size of the prize. An attractive young woman with a singer's voice announced the results to the animated crowd.

It was only a short walk from the downtown area where Satchel was staying to the ballpark, which sat at the Caribbean's edge. The view from home plate to right field provided a panorama of the ocean broken only by some palms. A constant breeze filled the ballpark with a fine ocean spray, which cooled the field. Behind left field was Calle Piña, where kids roamed during batting practice and ball games, hoping to snag a home run ball. What especially caught Satchel's eye when he first walked into the stadium was the sight of a rusty abandoned warship looming beyond the right-field fence.[10]

Seven thousand *fanáticos* impatiently waited for the three o'clock first pitch at the four-year-old stadium called the Campo Deportivo Municipal. Satchel was used to the Negro League stadiums with their gently curved stands studded with seats that slanted up a steep slope. It was odd he thought; this diamond "looked something like a bull ring." Especially once he realized "there are no bull fights down there."[11] The ninety-degree-angled colonial white structure shot straight up three layers like a wedding cake. Each layer was held up by square columns flush with the field. The dugouts along each foul line were like giant open bread boxes half buried in the foul territory dirt. The stadium just stopped at the end of each foul line—with Piña Street running behind left field and El Malecón, which skirted the Caribbean, beyond the right field.

Satchel's unease had grown steadily as he traveled about the island. Everything looked clean and the people well off—as long as he didn't stray too far from the places patrolled by the police. Yet just a few blocks away, peasants were living in poverty not unlike the poor black neighborhood full of shotgun houses that he had grown up in. And without fail when he went out late at night, he would be approached by bare-boned, barefoot children selling newspapers and lottery tickets.[12]

On game day before he left his club, Satchel soaked in a bath with water as hot as he could stand. He wouldn't get out until sweat was streaming down his forehead. After he toweled off, he carefully dressed in his thin white linen suit with sharp, shined black shoes. He surely kept thinking, "It's almost done." From that moment—until he pitched—he never stopped moving.

Satchel felt in his bones that today would be a high-pitched affair. He had known from the moment he landed that a "strong man" ran this country. Everywhere he went he saw the evidence: hosts of police officers and soldiers patrolling the streets with their flashy displays of guns, straps of ammunition, and knives.

When he arrived at the ballpark, limber, lean, six-feet-three Satchel went through his routine. First thing—to get all the muscles warm—he fielded bunts, hit balls to the infield, chased flies, worked out at third.[13] When he finally glanced up, he saw that every seat on the first two levels was filled. As he looked higher, he could see that even the third level was overflowing with *fanáticos* willing to stand for the entire game. Beyond the outfield fences a thick crowd was jostling for a view.

The manager called the Dragones together for what Satchel thought would be just a routine long-winded, empty pep talk. Instead he simply growled, "You better win."[14] As Satchel walked the length of the dugout, he hoped today he would only be needed to root for his teammates.

The *fanáticos* stood, roared, and waved their hats as the pin-striped Dragones took the field and their pitcher tossed his warmups. The sun, standing high over the third-base stands, cast short shadows of the batter, which fell toward first base.

As the game progressed, Satchel's nerves eased. His teammate from the Pittsburgh Crawfords, lefty Leroy Matlock, who had started the game, was cutting through the lineup of the Águilas Cibaeñas (Eagles of the Cibao Valley) using his great control to mix in sharp fastballs with curves, drops, screwballs, and sliders. He was coasting into the ninth with an 8–2 lead.

It was hard to tell if Matlock had run out of gas, if the hitters had figured him out, or if the sight of armed soldiers lined up in plain view had unnerved him, but he was suddenly hittable. In the twinkling of an eye, the championship game was in a state of collapse.

Single. Double. Single.

New York Cuban jumper and slick fielding first baseman David "Showboat" Thomas began the rally with a single for the Águilas. Then García doubled. Next "Big Splo" Spearman, another New York Cuban jumper, singled, cutting the lead to 8–3 with only one out and runners standing on first and third.

The manager stood, growled, and craned his neck to look down the length of the dugout to where Satchel was trying to keep out of sight. "Ven acá," he spat. In utter dread Satchel hastily warmed up and was soon summoned to pitch. As he walked to the mound, all he could think of were those soldiers standing in foul territory with long knives and guns in their belts—and the fact that "they could use them." The words "you better win" kept repeating in his head. Standing on the mound he felt so jittery that even as he talked to himself he was stuttering: "L-l-l-listen S-s-s-atch, pull yourself together before they air-condition you. You're just a few pitches away from riding a big bird back to the land of Uncle Sam." It was small comfort to the tall, lanky right-hander that anything he threw near the plate would be called a strike "'cause the umpires saw the guns too."[15]

Satchel's shattered nerves took a toll on his pitching. He quickly thought things through as clearly as he could. The first two hitters he would face were Pat Patterson and Santos Amaro. Because he had played with Patterson on the Pittsburgh Crawfords, he knew the speedy switch hitter could beat out almost any grounder to the hole. Next man up would be the tall, powerful, right-handed-hitting Cuban Santos Amaro. "El Canguro" was a different matter altogether. Satchel feared his power because he had already homered four times in this series.

Patterson touched Satchel for a single. When El Canguro came to the plate, he narrowed the lead to 8–5 with another single. Satchel finally got a break: he induced Philadelphia Star jumper "Red" Parnell to ground into a force at second.

Two outs.

The famous Cuban slugger Martín "El Maestro" Dihigo strode to the plate waving a bat in his hands. The sportswriter for *Listín Diario* later recounted what every *fanático* in the stadium was thinking: if the dangerous Dihigo, who led the league in homers and had hit three off Satchel got ahold of one, the game would be tied. With first base open, Satchel could walk Dihigo if he chose. Yet he decided to pitch to him.

Dihigo singled, driving in Pat Patterson for the sixth run. "Red" now stood at third. Dihigo took a healthy lead at first with his team down only two runs.

Standing on the mound, Satchel looked down at his feet. He closed his eyes for a split second to take stock. Everything felt okay but his stomach. A sick feeling kept growing down

TIME TO GET A JOB

there from knowing that the outcome of this game was bigger than baseball.

Because no matter who told him, "you better win," Satchel knew it originated from one source: the dictator Rafael Trujillo. From the moment he landed on the island, Satchel had heard the whispers about what happened to people who crossed Trujillo. Worse, the men who worked for Trujillo, men who he knew had, without hesitation, without remorse, killed other men, had told Satchel, "You better win."

3

Show Me the Money

Satchel looked down at his feet. He scratched at the mound dirt with the toes of his spikes: in a flash he took stock of it all. He felt a residue of doubt mixed with a pinch of regret. Yet he refused to regret the day he had taken the bankbook with his name above the ledger line and $30,000 right below.

He could remember that April day vividly. Two weeks earlier he had arrived in New Orleans—a city he had fallen in love with a decade earlier as a twenty-year-old. The circumstances of that first trip were slightly embarrassing: he had jumped his team at the offer of an old jalopy to play for the New Orleans Pelicans.

Satchel easily made friends wherever he went. Here in New Orleans he would listen to his friend Jelly Roll Morton effortlessly modulate between keys as he improvised with all the elements of jazz, syncopation, and blues. Here, dressed in his canary-yellow suit, Satchel joined his friends to eat, wander, and play all along South Rampart Street. They all knew Satch. Heads turned when he sauntered into the long-countered diners, honky-tonks, pool halls and theaters on the main drag—Dix's Barbershop, Pelican Billiard Hall, Tick Tock Tavern, King's Shoe Shine Parlor, Polmer Tailoring, Cohen's Loan & Jewelry Company, and Reiner's Pawn Shop. For blocks he could hear the melodious cries of street vendors selling pies, roasted corn, bread, cake, ice cream, sweet watermelon slices, waffles, and candy, along with an array of handymen selling services ranging from umbrella repair to knife sharpening.

Yet when Satchel headed south—even to a big city like New Orleans—he was coldly reminded by the others that he was just a "nigger." Even in New Orleans he could walk by but not into the central park. The streetcars had placards that were moved back and forth during the day to segregate the riders. They read:

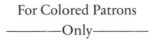

For Colored Patrons
————Only————

Just a few days after Satchel arrived in New Orleans, the talk suddenly modulated from a major key—girls, music, food, and baseball—to a minor one. Rapidly news spread that the previous day black Mississippians Roosevelt Townes and Robert McDaniels had been seized by a white mob while passing through the Grenada County jail yard on their way to be arraigned in court. Sheriff E. E. White had released his two black prisoners to the mob as he belly-laughed, remarking: "You have overpowered me boys."[1]

The mob pitched the two men into a waiting automobile, which they drove parade style down Highway 51. A caravan of 150 vehicles full of men, women, and children gleefully escorted the lead car. After traveling eleven miles, they reached the town of Duck Hill. There the mob stripped and bound Roosevelt Townes, gouged out his eyes with an ice pick, and burned him little by little with a plumber's blowtorch as the women held their children high to witness the man's agony. Next, the mob soaked him in gasoline and cheered as he burned. Robert McDaniels was stripped, flogged bloody, and told to run for his life. As he ran, he was riddled with buckshot from at least fifty shotguns.[2] As the mob rose to a fever pitch from torturing the two men, Everett Dorroh, a farmer who happened to be driving by, stopped to plead for the two men's lives. The good Samaritan was mobbed, tied to a tree, horsewhipped, shot in the legs, and "taunted by twenty-five or more children who were part of the mob."[3] Townes and McDaniels were the second and third lynching victims of

1937; eighteen-year-old Wes Johnson had been murdered by a mob two months earlier in Satchel's home state of Alabama.[4]

Confronted by newspaper reporters, the white sheriff had lied that he had been overpowered from behind so he "couldn't recognize any of the men."[5] Mississippi Governor Hugh White called the lynchings "absolutely inexcusable" but used them as an excuse to rail against federal antilynching legislation, saying that it would "be very costly to the state."[6] Louisiana Senator John Overton chimed in. "It does not require a lawyer," he lectured, "to know that Congress has no authority under our constitution to pass such a measure."[7]

Later that dark week a short man with sharp features, wearing a white linen suit and dark-banded fedora stopped Satchel on the sidewalk near the team's hotel. He introduced himself in proper English, flavored with a strong Spanish accent: "I'm Dr. José Enrique Aybar," he proclaimed. "I direct the baseball team in Ciudad Trujillo."[8]

Satchel stopped short. He looked quizzically at the little man. "I'd heard of sick clubs and ballplayers that looked pretty sick," he thought, "but I never knew there was one so sick it needed a doctor to manage it." "What can I do for you Doc?" he asked. "We are interested in your pitching. President Trujillo has instructed me to obtain the best pitcher possible for his team and our scouts recommend you."[9]

What Satchel didn't know was that Dr. Aybar had left for New Orleans at about the same time that he had. Only his journey had been far less relaxed than that of the ace pitcher.

His opening bid for Satchel was meant to awe. And it did.

The usually loquacious Paige stared down at the little doctor in disbelief mixed with a large helping of skepticism. Because he'd "been in a few deals like this," he remembered all those times when "everything gets said and everything gets promised and we all shake hands and have a drink and then everything kind of evaporates and all you wind up doing is staring at the damn room and the phone bill in the morning."[10]

Satchel looked dead into the dark eyes of the little doctor and asked if he "could see the money." At once Aybar made arrangements to meet the next day.[11]

The doctor punctually returned the next morning to hand Satchel a freshly minted bankbook with his name on it and thirty thousand dollars in it. It "sounded like thirty million," Satchel recalled.[12] He laid down one condition to Aybar: to also sign his friend, his chosen catcher Cy Perkins. Aybar quickly agreed to this demand even though he was in no need of a catcher.

This was a big bump in pay for a Negro League player in 1937—even Leroy "Satchel" Paige, the biggest star in the league, stood to make just a fraction of the doctor's offer. To a young man who as member of the semipro Mobile Tigers was paid one dollar per game or, if the team was short of money, a few gallons of lemonade, it was a fortune.

It had been a long journey from reform school to a place on the roster of the Mobile Tigers. When twelve-year-old Satchel was caught shoplifting a handful of brass rings from a local store, the police had summoned his mother to the police station before they would release him. Mother and son left with an order to appear first thing the next morning. Satchel expected her to be hopping mad, yet on their way home, his mother hugged him tightly and cried. Again he was surprised when they got home that his mother didn't get angry, didn't even spank him. She cried through the afternoon and the night. That next morning they made the trip together to the police station to meet with the state truant officer. The officer summarily sentenced Satchel to live out his adolescence at the Alabama Reform School for Juvenile Negro Law-Breakers in Mount Meigs.

The Mount Meigs institution had been built seven years earlier to tighten the grip of Alabama's apartheid state. Not surprisingly, it was just down the road from the state capital. The central campus was ringed by a series of long, rough-looking, poorly painted white board buildings with steep roofs, crowned by lightning rods and bookended by brick chimneys. Of the 281 acres, 125 were dedicated to farming. "Half a day is given to schoolroom instruction and half a day to manual work" was the reform school's credo.[13] "Instruction" was hardly up to the standards of even rural schoolhouses for there were but three teachers for 285 boys. Satchel's dormitory was cramped and had no indoor plumbing. Every night he was crammed into a single-wide bunk bed with three other boys.[14]

It was at this time that Satchel first fell in love with music. Right off he joined the Mount Meigs choir and soon became its leader. He enlisted as a drummer in the drum and bugle corps.[15] Every year after baseball was done, he spent much of his spare time singing.

Over the next five and one-half years, Satchel lived in the steady, structured world of the reform school. Even this regimen seemed a relief from the dissipation and poverty of black Mobile. "If I'd been left on the streets of Mobile to wander with those kids I'd been running around with," he recalled, "I'd of ended up as a big bum, a crook." "It gave me a chance to polish up my baseball game," he would later state; "it gave me some schooling I'd of never taken if I wasn't made to go to classes." "When you grow up as poor as me," even a place like Mount Meigs "can be mighty warm and good."[16]

The small, severely structured world of Mount Meigs allowed Satchel to master the art of pitching as taught by the school's baseball coach, Edward Byrd. Byrd taught him the basics: how to kick up his foot like "it was blacking out the sky" and how to swoop his arm around so it looked like he was letting the ball go when his "hand was right in the batters face."[17]

Always a showman, young Satchel boldly scribbled the word

"fastball" on the sole of his left shoe for opposing batters to see. "You know what's coming," his shoe taunted. "Let's see if you can hit it."[18]

At Mount Meigs Satchel began his lifelong habit of studying the knees of batters for signs of weakness. Standing on the mound he would watch their knees just "like a bullfighter watches a bull." When a batter swung, he could tell from how his knees moved exactly what his weaknesses were. Satchel discovered that this was the perfect way to put the ball where he knew the pitcher couldn't hit it.[19]

In December 1923 Satchel was released from reform school. The seventeen-year-old arrived back in Mobile, a young man determined to become a baseball star. Within days Satchel heard of a tryout for a local semiprofessional team. With pure chutzpah he showed up uninvited to the scheduled tryout. Patiently he waited for the last kid to be rejected before he stepped forward to pitch. Ten straight times he struck out the manager. When the sweaty, flummoxed man stopped swinging, he asked if Satchel "could throw fast consistently." An innocent smile came to Satchel's lips as he said, "No, sir, I do it all the time."[20]

4

Chapita

On a warm Friday evening in early spring, a group of powerful men began gathering at the opulent downtown law offices of Julio Cuello. Julio warmly welcomed each man as he arrived and promptly poured him a glass of brandy. Every man was wealthy, powerful, and a baseball *fanático*. The chief "Licey" patron arrived: Dr. José Enrique Aybar. After a while he was joined by top industrialist Francisco Martínez Alba, his counterpart for the rival Escogido.

"Gentlemen, gentlemen," Julio interjected once his guests had arrived, signaling an end to their small talk. Julio called the meeting to order. Underlying the pleasantries was a gnawing drive to erase the disappointment from their losses the previous season. Instead of engaging in a lengthy debate, they quickly agreed on a common purpose: to merge the two capital-city rivals into one team to win the championship. And so it was decided that the two capital-city teams—Los Tigres del Licey and Los Leonés del Escogido—would be blended into one, called Los Dragones de Ciudad Trujillo, the Dragons of Trujillo City.

In short order the men agreed that two other teams would play against the Dragones for the national championship: Las Estrellas Orientales (the Stars of the East), representing the sugar capital of the island, and Las Águilas Cibaeñas, representing the powerful ancient city to the north. They would play during the spring and summer in a series of weekend baseball games for the national championship. Of course the name of Trujillo must play the dominant role. The men decided to call the series *Campeonato por Reelección de Presidente Trujillo,* "Championship for the Reelection of President Trujillo."

Julio looked from face to face for unspoken permission to end things. At once a resolution was proposed and unanimously passed naming Rafael Trujillo the honorary president and protector of the team. Together the men rose out of respect for El Presidente and greeted the outcome with "enthusiastic applause."[1] It was left unsaid that the honorary president and protector of this newly minted baseball team did not even like baseball.

A dozen or so years earlier, the name Rafael Trujillo, if it had been uttered at all in such elegant offices of the capital city, would have elicited contempt. After all Rafael was little more than a country bumpkin who had grown up close by but worlds apart from the capital.

"Chapita, Chapita," the neighborhood kids had called as they ran through the streets looking for their friend Rafael. They had given him the nickname "Chapita" (bottle cap) because of his obsession for collecting flashy caps from soda and beer bottles and pinning the shiniest ones onto his shirt like a little general. As Rafael grew from child to teenager, his two older brothers smoothed his way by acting as his guide and introduced him to their circle of friends. Yet even with this extra boost, Rafael was somewhat a loner. Often he lost himself in long hikes up the twisting trails high into the mountains of the Cordillera Central to the north. He would marvel as he passed by isolated white-doored huts and through tiny villages until he reached Sabana de los Muertos.[2]

In those days the Trujillos lived in a small house off the main street. Rafael was the third son of José, a roving, good-natured, good-for-nothing merchant known to his neighbors as Don Pepe. His mother, the stout, stern Julia Molina, was the one who really ran the family. As he came of age, Rafael discovered that Don Pepe's grandmother was a mulatto and Julia's grandmother was the illegitimate daughter of a Haitian Army officer and a Haitian woman.[3] By then he also came to understand that black blood, while often an unspoken topic, could be a potent handicap to climbing his country's social ladder.

Chapita's San Cristóbal was a one-thousand-person hamlet tucked in the green coastal hills five miles from the Caribbean and fifteen from the capital. It had a main street with a scattering of homes up short side streets, all surrounded by tiny farms.[4] At one time it had been the center of a prosperous area but had slowly decayed after the collapse of the area's small sugar mills.[5] Chapita's education here totaled but five years, covering only the rudiments of reading, grammar, arithmetic, history, and writing. At school he was remembered solely for his obsession with neatness and orderliness.[6]

By sixteen Rafael had finished school. It was time to find a job. Young Rafael worked his meager family connections to land a job in the hot, cramped San Cristóbal telegraph office. There he learned the intricacies of telegraph communications from running telegrams to operating Morse code keys. It was only after Rafael swung a transfer to the telegraph office in the capital city, Santo Domingo, that he got his first taste of city living.[7]

Rafael was living in the capital city and had just turned twenty when the nation was stunned by the news that President Cáceres had been gunned down while taking his leisurely afternoon coach ride along El Malecón on a fall afternoon.[8] The president's assassination came after a hopeful period of stability for the country. Now everything was thrown back into an all-too-familiar pattern of chronic instability.

Suddenly Rafael lost his job as a telegraph operator. He was forced to return to San Cristobal. Now without the prospect of a decent job, he joined the La 44 gang, where he became fast friends with Miguel Ángel Paulino. Rafael and Miguel made money as members of La 44 by practicing an assortment of low-level crimes including thievery, blackmail, and graft.[9] Still Rafael refused to smoke, gamble, or drink heavily.

5

The Americans

The mid-August day was hot and dusty. Inside the insignificant rural church, everyone was perspiring except the groom. The Catholic priest looked into the eyes of twenty-one-year-old Rafael Trujillo Molina as he asked, "¿Quieres recibir por esposa a Aminta Ledesma Lachapelle prometes serle fiel, tanto en la prosperidad como en la adversidad, en la salud como en la enfermedad, amándola y respetándola durante toda su vida?"[1]

Rafael looked from the priest to his fourteen-year-old bride, Aminta Ledesma Lachapelle. He firmly replied, "Sí, quiero." She was not noticeably pregnant. But in San Cristóbal everyone knew. Aminta's parents were still fuming that she had taken up with one of the local hoods known as Chapita. They were only slightly consoled that he had been shamed into marrying their daughter.

Soon Chapita was able to buy a modest four-room home off the main street on Calle Padre Ayala in San Cristóbal for Aminta and his new daughter, Flor de Oro (Flower of Gold).[2] In the beginning he settled in the tiny home with his new family. But within a few years Chapita began spending less time there. At first it was because he was working at the sugar plantations to the east.

Luckily for Rafael, thuggery was just the experience needed for his next job as a private policeman on the sprawling sugar plantations, known as *ingenios*, just to the east of the capital city in San Isidro and Boca Chica.[3] Each of these *ingenios* had hundreds of poor workers—mainly Haitians—whom the companies controlled by leveraging them to the hilt, making them solely dependent on their employers for their money, housing, provisions, and food. Trujillo's job was to keep these thousands of poor workers in line with cajoling, threats, and of course violence when needed.

• • •

When Rafael was fifteen, U.S. president Teddy Roosevelt began issuing gunboat dictates to the Dominicans. At the time American financiers feared that the Dominican Republic was in imminent danger of defaulting on its large bond debt. So Roosevelt began applying intense pressure to the Dominican government in an effort to force it to allow Americans to take control of its revenue collection and dole out the proceeds to pay off its bond debt. He was successful. Roosevelt left only a small portion of Dominican government revenue available to support its own government.[4]

Rafael was twenty-four and a security guard at a sugar plantation when, in the summer of 1915, the U.S. Marines landed in the bordering country of Haiti. Quickly seizing control, the Americans seated a puppet president and took the reins of government and therefore complete control over the country's finances—all in order to rake off revenue to pay American bankers. Sensing a looming danger, the Dominican press raised the alarm with an editorial titled "The Godfathers," which warned, "The fire is getting close, and any spark may set off our powder."[5]

Suddenly, in the spring of 1916, American ally and Dominican president Juan Isidro Jiménez was lazing at his country villa when he caught wind of impeachment proceedings against him brewing in the capital. Losing no time Jimenez gathered a makeshift army to march on the capital. In sync U.S. Marines landed in Santo Domingo under the pretext of protecting U.S. citizens. Once they seized key positions, they sent word to Jiménez that they were ready to join forces with him to take back his government. Jiménez at first agreed, but after a fit of conscience he declined their offer, for he believed it was immoral to march against his own people using foreign troops.[6]

Still the marines remained in the capital. Still the Dominicans stood firm. To replace Jiménez they selected the broadly respected Francisco Henríquez y Caraval as their new president. Caraval was a practical man who let it be known that he was willing to allow the Americans to increase their role in his country's finances. He would even be willing to allow the Americans to act as a national police force. But the Americans demanded more, insisting on a legally binding decree turning over complete financial and military control. Caraval refused. In response the Americans choked off all revenue to the government, even to support essential services. Still the Dominicans stood firm. Government workers showed up to their jobs month after month to perform their duties without pay. During this period of flux, the Americans steadily built their presence by landing three new forces of marines from Haiti and Cuba.

By November 1916 the Americans had grown keenly aware that the Dominican Republic was on the brink of economic collapse. Worse yet they knew that if this occurred they would be blamed. Without notice the Marines marched on Santiago, which was then the political and economic power base of the country. On that same day the marines hoisted the U.S. flag over the old Spanish Fort Ozama in the capital. By capturing the two principal cities, the Americans had seized control of the country.

Finally, on November 29, 1916, a little over a month after Rafael turned twenty-five, U.S. Marine captain Harry S. Knapp issued a "proclamation of occupation" from the flagship *Olympia*, pronouncing an American military dictatorship. In rapid-fire succession Captain Knapp issued executive orders requiring full censorship of the press, abolishing free elections, suspending the existing congress, firing the foreign ministers, and expressly outlawing the possession of firearms, munitions, or explosives by Dominicans.[7]

The severe, clear-eyed, walrus-mustached Knapp worked with stern marine efficiency to stanch the flow of arms. Within days he canceled all existing gun permits and required Dominican citizens to turn in their weapons. Between outright confiscations a door-to-door search for arms, and voluntary turn-ins, the marines seized over three million firearms. With a population of just over eight hundred thousand, this represented an eye-popping three-plus guns for every man, woman, and child in the country. The marines dumped the guns in the ocean.[8]

In short order Knapp disbanded and abolished all Dominican military forces. He replaced them with a newly formed Guardia Nacional Dominicana. Simultaneously he ordered the construction of an extensive network of modern roads so that his forces could speed to any corner of the island where a disturbance might break out. Within days the Americans seized the customs houses in the major ports to take full control of the Dominican Republic's finances. Control was turned over to American functionaries; this guaranteed American banks and financiers repayment of the millions in debt owed to them by the Dominican government.

Now under the boot of an American military dictatorship, the country settled into a state of docility. The one remaining emotional outlet for Dominican's nationalism was the baseball rivalry between the U.S. Marines and the Dominican teams. During the years of American occupation, these games were closely followed throughout the country, and wins against the Americans were a source of great national pride. It can be said that during the American occupation baseball sank deep roots in the national soul, which in time led to the blossoming of professional baseball.

Signing up native recruits for Captain Knapp's new Guardia Nacional Dominicana turned out to be no easy feat. Many

Dominicans simply felt it was unpatriotic to aid the American dictatorship.

In the second year of the American occupation, Rafael announced to Aminta that he would be going away to soldier for the invading Americans. As it turned out, running a security operation for a large sugar plantation was just the sort of experience the marines needed. Years later Rafael would point to this moment as the point when he found his calling, the event that gave his life both passion and purpose.

Wearing his woolen uniform with its flat, taut collar, Second Lieutenant Trujillo looked out with dark large irised eyes framed by cropped wavy black hair; small, low-placed, slightly protruding ears; lips topped with a cupid's bow; a clipped mustache with side margins; and at the bottom a vague, soft chin. Marine training and discipline appealed to the young man's innate sense of orderliness. Young Lieutenant Trujillo was punctual, obedient, and efficient. Above all his uniform was permanently spotless and crisp, his shoes were impeccably shined, and his brass buttons and insignia blazed.

On his first efficiency report, Lieutenant Trujillo received excellent marks for "military bearing" and "cleanliness of person and uniform" and was praised for his "way of wearing uniform and care of same."[9] The Americans also took note of his "initiative, intelligence and good judgment." One reporting officer wrote: "I consider this Officer one of the best in the service."[10]

The rule of the marines under Captain Knapp was thoroughly repressive yet relatively bloodless. Three years into the occupation, Admiral Thomas Snowden took over. Suddenly the climate grew repressive and violent. Now the marines with their new Dominican police contingent found themselves fighting against bands of insurgents (the Americans called them bandits) in the eastern provinces of the island. In response they began to employ increasingly brutal tactics, at times even burning whole villages to the ground. All too often they shot suspects when they sensed the slightest resistance. To extract information from uncooperative citizens, they tied ropes around their heads and turned them with levers until the information sought was squeezed out of the victim.[11] It is unclear if young Rafael learned this technique from the marines or in fact taught it to them.

After seven years of occupation, the American public grew troubled by the cost and brutality of the operation. The United States initiated negotiations with the Dominicans, which largely revolved around demanding guarantees of debt repayment. Free elections were at last held in 1924, and sixty-three-year-old former president Horacio Vásquez was elected in a landslide. The chore of keeping order in the new democracy was turned over to the American-trained and recruited but fully Dominican Guardia Nacional.

Rafael clearly saw that the military represented his only ladder of opportunity. Right from the start the marines moved him from city to city. When he reached the eastern agricultural city of El Seibó in 1920, it was as Second Lieutenant Trujillo, not a man, he felt, to be married to a simple country girl. So Second Lieutenant Trujillo began looking. He mixed and mingled with the cattle ranchers and sugar growers who made up the "better" families of El Seibó. To impress the locals he used one of the flags from the glorious 1844 revolution to lead a showy civic flag raising on Dominican Independence Day.[12] In time Second Lieutenant Trujillo took a liking to Bienvenida Morel, the daughter of one of the local worthies, Don Servando Morel. Yet when he applied for her hand in marriage and for membership in the city's finest social club, he was promptly rejected from both by his betters.[13]

Spurned by his fellow countrymen, Trujillo was nevertheless embraced by the Americans. He left El Seibó in August 1921 for intensive training by the U.S. Marines at the new Haina Military Academy, halfway between the capital and his hometown.[14] Because the Americans valued Trujillo as a soldier, they helped him rapidly climb the military ladder of opportunity: 1922, captain; 1924, major; 1924, lieutenant colonel; 1925, colonel; 1927, brigadier general.[15]

Married but still in pursuit of a socially superior marriage, Lieutenant Colonel Trujillo set his sights on a young woman from the northern city of Monte Cristi. She was the daughter of the respectable Buenaventura Ricardo Heureaux. Nine months after his appointment as lieutenant colonel, Trujillo was granted a divorce from Aminta of San Cristóbal.[16] After all, as the American foreign minister's wife later put it, Aminta was "just a peasant woman and he got rid of her very early."[17]

Bienvenida Ricardo was an ideal partner: an appealing young lady who possessed social standing yet lacked wealth. Colonel Trujillo showered her with expensive gifts. He turned on his romantic charm until she agreed to their marriage over her family's objections.

Rafael Trujillo Molina once again solemnly uttered, "Sí, quiero," only this time to a lawyer instead of a priest. After the civil ceremony the families, along with friends of the bride and groom, filtered into the dining hall for toasts and wedding cake. The colonel had spent considerable time dreaming up a way to win over the aristocratic crowd. He was determined to make "una impresión." That night he approached the wedding cake—a high-class confection covered with handmade sugar flowers, lace, angels, and figurines. With a flourish the colonel cast aside the tiny cake cutter and drew a gold sword from his scabbard. He commandingly cut into the cake. At his first slash the cake crashed to the floor with a dull thud.[18]

• • •

August 16, 1927, marked the sixty-fourth National Day of Remembrance for the Restoration of the Republic. Opposite the ancient cathedral on Parque Colon, a regiment of Trujillo's troops acted as honor guard to the president and members of the legislative and judicial branches. They stood in columns and listened as a solemn Te Deum was sung in thanksgiving for the liberty they now enjoyed.

Accompanied by drumrolls and sharp bugle calls, Trujillo's troops paraded toward the palace of the president. A thin rain began falling. As they marched, the wind picked up and the rain turned heavy. Still Trujillo's regiment pushed ahead to the presidential mansion to present the nation's colors to President Vásquez.

Trujillo's regiment stood at attention in full formation, as President Vásquez announced his military appointments. That evening, with great ceremony, the president pinned the insignia of brigadier general on Rafael Trujillo's uniform.[19]

Four days after being named brigadier general, Trujillo's military magazine, *La Revista*, reassured the nation that there was no need to fear the emergence of a powerful military with Trujillo at its head. After all the general had learned "discipline and civic spirit" in a time of peace. He would not become a "Caesar, Alexander the Great, and Napoleon" who "later abused their authority."[20]

General Trujillo played on national pride as he conducted an intense lobbying campaign to convince the president and the national congress to transform his brigade into something the Americans had abolished during their occupation: a national army.[21] With this act signed into law, Rafael became brigadier general of the national army.

6

A Long, Lanky Black Boy by the Name of Satchell

One-dollar-a-game Satchel kept his eyes peeled for the next big thing. It took him two years of playing with the semipro Mobile Tigers and other local teams to get his first taste of professional ball. His big chance was given to him in the spring of 1926 by Mobile native and owner-manager of the Chattanooga White Sox Alex Herman.[1]

It didn't take long for Herman to discover that signing a contract with his young player would be "tougher than a no-hitter" because the signature on this contract had to come from Mrs. Paige. Herman knew from his friends that she was a feisty, protective mom—no one was going to take the slightest advantage of her son. Satchel's eyes widened as he listened to his mom dictate a list long enough to "take care of an army."[2] Mrs. Paige agreed to sign Satchel's contract only after Herman promised to send the lion's share of his fifty-dollars-a-month salary home to the family and to enforce her list of dictates.

Herman took his responsibility to Satchel's mom seriously. As the team's bus rattled into Chattanooga, Satchel's teammates asked him out for dinner. He had no choice but to glumly inform them he was having dinner with the manager. As for playing cards or carousing, well there was the matter of that 9:30 p.m. curfew.[3] And then there was that matter of his big feet. Herman couldn't find any baseball shoes in Satchel's size in town so "spikes had to be nailed to his street shoes until some size-12, triple-A baseball shoes could be found."[4]

Opening day for the Chattanooga White Sox fell on the last

day of April 1926. This glorious spring day was kicked off by a parade through the streets of Chattanooga. Herman's White Sox gathered in front of the Elks Club on Pine Street—they marched down Ninth to Market and ended at Palmetto Street across from the ballpark—all the while accompanied by the Duncan's Syncopators. Club president Trimble threw out the first pitch to Dr. McIntosh, the "exalted ruler of the colored Elks."[5]

Before his debut Satchel was listed in the *Chattanooga Times* as "Page." The next day, and forever after, it was "Satchell." (In the paper that day his name appeared in the two "l" form; this version was used almost as often as the one "l" version throughout his life.)

Satchel became an immediate sensation. The local paper raved about "the airtight pitching of a long, lanky black boy by the name of Satchell."[6] It reported that the powerful Barons "were held down at the bat by the mysterious curves of Pitcher Satchell. Darris, at short for the Barons, was the only Alabamian who could solve the long Satchell."[7] The team Satchel shut down wearing his improvised spikes went on to win the pennant of the Negro Southern League.[8]

Soon the *Chattanooga Times* enthused that Satchel's team was "drawing big crowds of both colored and whites." To be helpful the reporter wrote that henceforth there would be "a special section of the Andrews field stands . . . reserved for white fans."[9]

Just a little more than a week into the season, the rookie pitcher was singled out as the "ace" of the White Sox staff. In a game shortened by darkness, Satchel gave a pitching performance that foreshadowed his greatness. Facing the Atlanta Black Crackers, he struck out nine batters in six innings, including three straight in the second inning, allowing just two hits and no runs. The *Chattanooga Times* compared him to former Major League star Rube Waddell, who was revered for his blazing fastball and superb control.[10]

As the season progressed, Manager Herman worked hard to

perfect Satchel's pinpoint control. Under the manager's keen eye, Satchel pitched balls through a hole the size of a hat in a fence. He learned to knock over bottles lined up near home plate.[11] Satchel would often show off his preternatural control by placing a bubble-gum wrapper over home plate with great ceremony and then consistently throwing a ball over the wrapper. In later years he entertained crowds before barnstorming games by driving four nails through a board held behind home plate with fewer than ten pitches.[12]

After posting a 4 and 4 record during its opening home stand, Satchel's team set out for a road trip on a rickety old school bus. As the team rolled down the primitive Tennessee roads, the players felt every bump, every thud from the potholes clear up their spines. The roads were the easy part. The challenge was finding gas stations and restaurants that would serve "coloreds" or let them use a bathroom. Before leaving on any road trip, Herman spent hours calling friends to compare notes so that he could plot a route with enough such stops. In some rural areas this was simply impossible; the men were forced to make due by packing large amounts of food so they could eat on the bus. For bathrooms they had to find out-of-the-way fields.

About an hour after dark fell, the White Sox team bus rolled straight through Memphis to the ballpark. After the bus parked, Herman hollered, "Everybody out." Rookie Satchel, however, stayed seated. A few minutes later the coach came looking for him only to find Satchel still sitting on the bus. "Just have that driver take me to the hotel where we're staying," Satchel suggested. "Staying?" Herman laughed. "This is where you're staying Satch. You think we can afford staying in a hotel."[13]

Using their suitcases for pillows, Satchel and his teammates slept on the ball field that night. Only as they played more games were they able save enough money to stay in hotels. In those days many towns in the Deep South had no hotels for "coloreds." In those places Herman was forced to impose on friends or relatives to put up his team.

• • •

On that first road trip Satchel's team won five games and lost seven, but it was Satchel's performance that the *Chattanooga Times* singled out for praise: "The lanky right-hander, made a great record on the trip, setting down all opposition."[14]

It wasn't long before Satchel took note of the large number of fans who paid to see him pitch. He went to his manager and asked for a pay raise from fifty to one hundred dollars. From that day on, both his power to draw fans and his skill to draw money from his team's owners never subsided. Money meant newfound freedom for Satchel. At six feet three and 140 pounds, he mostly got away with eating ice cream and cake yet still struggled to put on extra weight. Upon pocketing his first big baseball paycheck, he vanished for two days to buy new clothes, a steak, a shotgun, and a bottle and went "looking for a gal."[15]

Word of Satchel's talent spread rapidly. In the middle of his second season with the Chattanooga White Sox, Herman was able to sell his contract to the powerful Birmingham Black Barons of the Negro National League. This represented a real jump in competition, as the Black Barons were the elite team of black professional baseball in the South.

Before his first game with the Black Barons, Satchel sauntered onto the field in Birmingham to shake hands with Cy Perkins, his new catcher. "There ain't no needs for signs, I guess," Satchel remarked nonchalantly. "I don't take them too good. Anyway, I'm the easiest guy in the world to catch. All you have to do is show me a glove and hold it still. I'll hit it." Satchel smiled when he noticed Cy's "this-guy-is-a-little-nuts" look and politely asked two players to hold bats about six inches apart in front of home plate. Satchel fired pitch after pitch between their bats right into Cy's mitt.[16]

Cy and Satchel came to know and trust each other as only catchers and pitchers can. In no time they became fast friends—with the proviso that Satchel would always be number one.

It was during those early years that Satchel began his lifelong love affair with the automobile. One summer he jumped from his team for a few weeks to pitch in New Orleans in exchange for an "old jalopy." He soon jumped back to his original team and was forgiven.[17]

On an April day, eleven years later, standing on a New Orleans street with $30,000 in his hands, Satchel Paige got ready to make the biggest jump of all.

7

Trujillo Es El Jefe

Opportunity came sooner than Trujillo expected. Clumsily President Vásquez tried to tack an extra two years on to his term in office without holding an election. This blunder quickly wore away any patina of democratic fair play and wrecked his popularity. To make matters worse, in the midst of Vásquez's self-inflicted political predicament, the old president fell ill. He was forced to travel to Johns Hopkins Medical Center in Baltimore to undergo surgery to remove one of his kidneys.

General Trujillo smelled weakness and saw opportunity. Immediately he cast around for a partner. Soon he found his man in Estrella Ureña, a vainglorious yet mediocre politician with outsized aspirations who had built a power base in the critical Santiago region.

With Ureña signed on, General Trujillo put his plan into motion. Once the old, sick president returned from the United States, the general went out of his way to pantomime abject loyalty, while allowing Ureña to secretly gather a band of rebels in Santiago. Trujillo told Ureña that once he had gathered his men he would supply them with arms and allow them to march unmolested into the capital city, where they would proclaim a new government. Further the general promised that he would straightaway proclaim his support for Ureña and have him installed as president of the Dominican Republic.

General Trujillo had learned from the Americans the importance of controlling the means of violence. He carefully supplied Ureña's rebels with a collection of obsolete, second-rate arms. They were so bad that the politician's forces were found at kilometer 30, "complaining bitterly about the condition of their weapons."[1]

As the ragged, poorly armed rebels marched toward Santo Domingo, President Vásquez was repeatedly warned by his friends that he had been betrayed by his general. The president stubbornly refused to heed the rumors, instead insisting on a face-to-face meeting with his general.

Earlier that week Trujillo had holed up in his military command center at Fortaleza Ozama, a castle-like fortress built on the west bank of the Ozama River by the Spanish in 1505. President Vásquez anxiously flooded Trujillo with entreaties to meet. But his general kept pushing off the requests, claiming that he was too ill. Out of desperation the old president simply drove to the fortress and insisted on a face-to-face meeting with his sick general. As the president's motorcade approached the fortress, Trujillo's soldiers stopped his cars at the gate and only allowed the president's car to pass.

Like a child feigning illness to stay home from school, Trujillo acted as if he had just risen from bed and made himself look sweaty and weak. When the distressed president came face-to-face with the general, he received nothing but disarming reassurances of his loyalty. On the spot General Trujillo dispatched a unit of troops under the command of a Vásquez loyalist with stern orders to quell the rebellion. Moments after the president's exit, the general dispatched another party of troops loyal to him with countermanding orders to dislodge the Vásquez loyalist—if necessary, to shoot him.

Soon Ureña's forces flooded unchecked into the capital city. Brandishing their antique weapons, they occupied all the key positions. Ureña loudly demanded a new government. That was the moment that President Vásquez knew his general had betrayed him. Under pressure from the United States, Vásquez had Ureña appointed third in succession. Then Vásquez and his vice president resigned. This allowed Ureña to occupy the presidential chair by succession. In cutting this deal the Americans explicitly barred Trujillo from running for president in the upcoming May elections.

Straightaway the new ex-president and his ex–vice president fled to Puerto Rico. Without missing a beat Trujillo ordered his troops to seize back all the second-rate guns he had supplied to the rebels, leaving President Ureña holding the titular power while Trujillo held the firepower.

Within days Trujillo announced he would be running as a candidate for president in the May elections. All President Ureña could muster was a weak complaint to the American legation. The Americans meekly refused to enforce their verbal agreement. A few weeks later Trujillo called Ureña into his office to order his resignation. Ureña resigned. On the spot Trujillo downgraded him to a candidate for vice president on the Trujillo ticket. Dr. Jacinto Peynado, a trusted friend, was named to the position of caretaker president.

There would be no vulgar military coup. Trujillo insisted on a patina of legality no matter how preposterous it all looked. His method for winning the election was quite simple. He hurriedly reconstituted his La 44 gang and put his old gangmember friend, Miguel Ángel Paulino, in command. Their mission was to unleash a reign of terror intended to crush any existing or nascent opposition. Paulino rechristened the gang La 42—an ominous tip of the hat to the Forty-Second Marine Company, which had earned a reputation for extreme brutality during the American occupation.[2]

Within days of Trujillo's announcement, Paulino, with his tight-knit band of gangsters, toured the country in a shiny red Packard with plates reading "La 42." His gang pulled into cities, stopped at the houses of key opponents, knocked on their doors, and gunned them down, only to drive on to the next city unmolested. Often they would pull up next to an enemy standing on a street corner and gun him down in broad daylight. Paulino's red Packard became known among the terrorized citizenry as the "Carro de la Muerte," "the Car of Death."

Naked violence reached a crescendo when Trujillo's thugs ambushed the motorcade carrying many of the opposition candidates just outside Santiago. Miraculously the politicians escaped without loss of life. Yet when they finally stopped, two former cabinet members traveling with the group found bullet holes in their clothes.[3]

The terror unleashed by Captain Miguel Ángel Paulino's La 42 touched every rung of society. An American observer of the election reported that "the Presidential campaign witnessed the death or mysterious disappearance of a great number of his [Trujillo's] opponents. These included former cabinet ministers, ex-Senators, leading politicians, journalists, ranchers, businessmen, students and labor leaders."[4]

Eventually opposition leaders petitioned the Junta Central Electoral (Central Election Board) to order a fair election. Now nine days before the election, and unwilling to take on Trujillo, the junta resigned en masse. Immediately Trujillo's friend and acting president, Jacinto Peynado, replaced the members of the junta with handpicked stooges.[5] This move was then challenged in the court of appeals. Soon it was discovered that a verdict finding these appointments illegal was about to be read in open court. Within minutes Paulino's machine-gun-toting gang seized control of the courtroom. The justices of the court of appeals hastily adjourned, never to be heard from again.[6]

Even in the face of Trujillo's thugs, citizens resisted. Members of the Chauffeur's Union took to the streets of the capital to oppose Trujillo's election. They held a rally in the heart of the city at Independence Park, where they passed out leaflets branding Trujillo a "cattle thief." Within moments a group of soldiers accompanied by members Paulino's gang appeared in the park to gun down the demonstrators. After the gunplay

Paulino, with his gun-toting thugs in tow, sauntered down the street and burst into the Chauffeur's Union hall. On the spot Paulino had himself voted into office as president of the union by acclamation.[7]

One individual who did keep speaking up against Trujillo was Dr. José Enrique Aybar. Aybar was a well-known local dentist who doubled as a political orator. Trujillo must not have taken Aybar seriously, for he did nothing to stop him. The little dentist delivered fiery speeches against Trujillo denouncing his movement as one that had "served only to abort a candidate who, like the fruit of all abortion, ha[d] no vitality." Aybar always ended his anti-Trujillo speeches by shouting, "No puede ser!" (It cannot be!). "No puede ser!" became the *grito* (rallying cry) of the opposition.[8] We will never know if it was all prearranged, but immediately after the election Dr. Aybar underwent a full public conversion to become one of the staunchest loyalists in Trujillo's constellation.

Trujillo was too clever to rely solely on guns and thuggery. He amassed notable support from the vast majority of the captains of industry, religious leaders, jurists, politicians, and young intellectuals. After all, these leaders reasoned, this election was being conducted no differently from many others they had lived through—it was more or less business as usual.

When Election Day, May 16, 1930, arrived, voters streamed to the polls to cast their ballots for president. When they entered their polling places, they were stunned to discover soldiers, not civilians, running the election. Early that night the new central electoral board emphatically reported that Rafael Trujillo had received 223,731 votes against only 1,883 votes for his opposition, representing over 99 percent of the vote.[9] Trujillo called his movement a *movimiento cívico*, "civic movement." In whispered tones it was renamed a *movimiento cínico*, "cynical movement."[10]

Jarringly, at four in the morning on August 16, 1930, the citizens of Santo Domingo were awakened by the sound of reveille being played from the city gates. Soon military bands began marching through the city streets, which had been lined with soldiers in dress uniforms and decked out with newly strung electric lights and triumphal arches.

"My coronation" is how Trujillo referred to his inauguration as president. And so it must have felt, when at ten o'clock sharp, General Rafael Trujillo slowly ascended the inaugural platform, dressed in an impeccably tailored military uniform, complete with gold epaulettes, medals that would have produced envy in a French field marshal, all topped off with a tricolored sash decorated with the Dominican coat of arms. On his head sat the plumed bicorne of the nineteenth-century black dictator Ulises Heureaux, who was infamous for his brutality.[11] On one occasion Heureaux had invited his brother-in-law for dinner. After dinner the dictator inquired how his brother-in-law had enjoyed the meal. "Very well" was his answer. To which the dictator casually replied, "I am glad of that for I am about to have you shot."[12]

Just days after Trujillo's inauguration, the sky darkened, and a steady downpour turned into driving rain. The people of Santo Domingo felt the air growing heavy in their bones.

Hurricane San Zenón struck the heart of the capital city. A little before noon the storm hit land. The Caribbean crashed over the breakwater, El Malecón. Waves surged inland as far as the second street, where they rhythmically uprooted the homes, carrying away the structures with everyone in them. Sheets of steel torn from roofs were sent flying through the air like playing cards. Many of those who wandered outside were decapitated or sliced in half by the flying sheets of metal.[13] As the storm progressed, trees were ripped from the ground while others had their crowns casually snapped off as if by a giant. This first wave of destruction lasted half an hour.

Without warning a calm descended on the city as the eye of the hurricane passed over. Air pressure plummeted. People's ears felt ready to burst. It became almost too easy to take a breath. Ten minutes later the storm regained its fury, only this time with the winds savagely blowing in the opposite direction. Suddenly the water mains burst, flooding the already-drenched city. Destruction was nearly total. Of the city's ten thousand buildings, only four hundred were left standing, all in the colonial district. There were eight thousand casualties, with two thousand dead, and six thousand injured.[14]

Quickly crews were assembled to haul the drenched corpses of the hurricane victims to the Plaza Columbina, where they were stacked in great mounds. Captain Miguel Ángel Paulino, Trujillo's trusted friend from his gang days, rushed into action. He ordered hundreds of prisoners, many of them political opponents, shot. Hurriedly their bodies were hauled down to the plaza and piled onto the mounds of rapidly rotting corpses. Next Paulino procured a large quantity of gasoline, which he had his men pour on the pyres of bodies and ignite.[15] The bonfire of corpses along the shore of the Caribbean lit up the night sky and filled the air with the stench of burning flesh and hair.[16] "This speedy action," President Trujillo proclaimed, "has saved our country from a horrible plague."[17]

So complete was the devastation that it was now possible to birth a new city. Detritus was cleared away. Slums, which had been simply erased, were to be replaced in the outskirts. As they were rebuilt, the poor were threatened with jailing if the exterior of their meager homes was kept anything but tidy. Streets were rethought and repaved. Palms were replanted. El Malecón was rebuilt and widened.

As the residents rebuilt their homes, the smart ones chose to display a brass plaque reading: "En esta casa Trujillo es el jefe" (In this house Trujillo is the boss).

8

Opening Day Away

Before he knew it, Dr. José Enrique Aybar was swept up in the hurly burly of opening day. He began by ordering fitted uniforms to be designed in the image of the New York Yankees—pinstripes, except with subtle V-neck cuts. Emblazoned across the chest of the shirts was script reading "C. Trujillo" with a flourish worthy of John Hancock underneath. After picking the fabric, he had his player's measurements taken. Aybar sent them out to be sewn by a local seamstress on her trusty Singer. Black belts, spikes, and calf-high white socks with three thick horizontal stripes completed the uniform.

The laundered, ironed uniforms were delivered to Aybar's capital-city office along with a horde of bats and balls. He then hired a bus and phoned ahead to book hotel rooms in the sugar capital of the island.

The night before the team's debut, Dr. Aybar toiled over his speech for the pregame ceremonies of Sunday's opening game. When it was finished to his satisfaction, he stood before a large mirror and practiced. The man who looked back at him was of below average height with receding jet-black hair, a light Spanish complexion, and a small, straight, unsmiling mouth overshadowed by a long, wide nose.

Early the following morning, Aybar dressed in his tropical white suit, crisp white cotton shirt with a thickly knotted, broad red tie and donned a white fedora with a wide black band. He rushed off to meet his Dragones for their first road trip. At the bus were five Cuban players and a single Puerto Rican. Three

Dominicans and a collection of subs were the stragglers, who arrived separately, some late.

Before leaving, Dr. Aybar ordered the team bus packed with the equipment, uniforms, *aperitivos*, and water. The dentist and his players filed onto the bus late Saturday to set off on the forty-nine-mile drive to the rival city. A few minutes later they crossed the bright-white bridge over the Ozama River that had replaced the one swept away by the hurricane. It was a thoroughly modern structure lined with sleek gooseneck electric-light standards. As the bus rolled east, it mainly hugged the Caribbean coast of the island but at times wandered inland.

After riding a few hours on the rough road, the players found themselves surrounded by a sea of windblown sugarcane. Periodically they rolled by the small camps, known as *bateys*, of the field hands. When they finally approached San Pedro de Macorís, they could see the cane pushing for miles up into the hills. In the distance loomed the sugar *ingenios* with their small-gauge railroads, bodegas, *bateys*, and massive factories where the sugar was milled and cooked. Toward the end of the trip, they came to the wide Higuamo River. They marveled as they crossed the newly built Ramfis suspension bridge. In just a few more minutes, their bus came to a stop in the country's sugar capital.

Two decades earlier San Pedro de Macorís had been the Caribbean boomtown floating on the enormous rise in sugar prices after World War I. A steroid-like growth spurt had urbanized the city's core with mansions for sugar barons (some, unusual for the time, made of reinforced concrete), a new church dedicated to San Pedro the apostle, an ornate fire station, streetcars, and a broad *malecón* that skirted the river and the sea.[1] The city had even opened an opera house at which Jenny Lind sang.

Once the Dragones settled into their hotel, the players wandered down to the central square, past the large white cathedral and a gingerbread fire station, and then to the *malecón* before stopping for dinner. The breeze, which had been blowing from the Caribbean, switched directions and now blew off the hills to the north.

Dr. Aybar woke early on Sunday morning to notice that the city was already swarming with cars, carriages, and fans from all parts of the country, many in search of an early *desayuno* (breakfast) with *café con leche* (coffee with milk) before the nine o'clock game.

Throngs of field hands and mill workers, a large number with their families, were making their way into town. Many were walking. Others took the family burro. The men wore their best white cotton pants and shirts, while the women wore bright-colored print dresses. As they streamed toward the stadium, everyone excitedly chatted with his or her neighbors about the stars they would see play today for their beloved Estrellas Orientales, the defending national champions.

Over a month earlier a group of these *fanáticos* had gathered at a pier inside the sheltered mouth of the Higuamo River. They had glanced at their watches while listening intently for the sound of propellers. Suddenly out of the western sky, they saw a speck; soon they heard the dull roar of a Sikorsky s-40 flying boat. The Pan American pilot veered south to make a wide right-hand turn into the mouth of the river. Water was sent shooting into the air as the flying boat skidded to a stop on the calm waters of the river. At once a boat was sent to take a passenger off the floating ramp, which had been lowered into the water.

It hadn't taken long for the boat to come near enough to the pier for them to see the short, stocky frame of Manual "Cocaína" García, a black Cuban pitcher whom they remembered fondly for his heroics in last year's championship run.[2] Federico Nina, the president of the Las Estrellas Orientales, stepped forward to welcome Cocaína back to his city.[3] Cocaína would be joined by five other Cuban stars brought into the country before the team played its first game.

The names of Cuban players were on many of the sugar

workers' tongues as they walked to the stadium on the day of the first game. But it was their Dominican hero, Juan "Tetelo" Vargas—they knew him simply as "Tetelo"—whom everyone was talking about. Indeed, they were walking to a newly built five-thousand-seat ballpark that had recently been renamed Campo Deportivo Tetelo Vargas after their thirty-year-old star.[4]

Fanáticos swarmed the ticket windows. Those standing near the entrance gates were assaulted by the bellowing of ticket scalpers, cushion vendors, and hawkers of seemingly every food and drink that could be carted about for sale. *Fanáticos* crushed into the stands early to excitedly watch the players take turns at batting and fielding practice. They were especially eager to see their three new Cuban additions, Blanco, Rojo, and Oms, whom the crowd observed closely during warmups.

Promptly at 9:00 a.m. a group of dignitaries ambled onto the velvet-green field. Local team president Nina read a pleasant speech that Dr. Aybar politely replied to with pretentious remarks. Two beautiful women strolled onto the field, Anita Santoni and Miss Esperanza Guerra, and each proudly hoisted the flag of her home team.

Shortly after the speeches and flag raisings, leaders of each team and sportswriters were joined by an assortment of sports personalities in the middle of the field. Throwing out the first ball for the Campeonato por Reelección de Presidente Trujillo was the director of the National Immigration Service, Raul Carbuccia.

Soon the groundskeepers finished raking the infield, smoothing it so that not even a pebble showed. Captains of the teams strode onto the field for a short conference with the umpires near the foul line as they delivered their team's lineup. Then the umpires scattered to their stations. After adjusting his shin guards and chest protector, the home-plate umpire shouted for play to begin.

A roiling roar surged from the crowd. Everyone rose. The

men waved their hats as the Estrellas took the field wearing their darkly pinstriped uniforms with "ORIENTE" printed in a mild arch across the chest, black belts, black stirrups, and white hats with a black brim. Instead of diminishing the roar rather grew into an unceasing jumble of groans, cheers, curses, yelps, and boos, for nearly everyone was a gambler who was wagering nonstop on pitches, batters, outcomes of innings, errors, scores, and combinations of it all. Bets were yelled and hand signaled. Sweaty bills were passed back and forth between each pitch accompanied by jeering, cheering, and barking.

The Estrellas' lineup was loaded with Cuban and Dominican stars. At first base was the Cuban Carlos Blanco, a right-handed .300 hitter with good defensive skills. At second was the Dominican Ramón "Món" Ruiz. Filling out the infield at short was Aladino Páez with the Cuban Luis "Pedro" Arango at third. The masterful Cuban Ramon "El Profesor" Bragaña had been tapped to be the opening-day pitcher. Bragaña's battery mate was the tough-as-nails Cuban Julio Rojo. Ultra-fast Dominican Juan "Tetelo" Vargas roamed center and anchored the Estrellas' outfield. Cuban stars Alejandro "El Caballero" Oms played right and Manuel "Cocaína" García was in left.[5]

The six-foot Cuban mulatto "El Profesor" Bragaña took the mound for the Estrellas. He mixed his lively fastball with a sharp curve to quickly set the Dragones down in the top of the first.

Cuban right-hander Silvio García then walked to the mound for the Dragones—the same Silvio García who, years later, when being vetted by Branch Rickey as the possible first black to play in the Majors, was asked what he would do if an opposing player hurled a racial epithet at him, calmly replied: "I would kill him."[6] García quickly shut down the side by striking out Tetelo and Món Ruiz with well-placed fastballs.[7]

Each team pushed across a run in the second inning. But the tie wasn't broken until the bottom of the fifth, when the Estrellas scored a run to grab a 2–1 lead.

As it turned out, the brilliant work of Dragones pitcher Silvio García was spoiled by four errors, which led to a 4–1 loss in the morning game.

The fans of the sugar capital filed noisily out of the stadium, enthusing about the victory as they headed for their *almuerzo* (lunch). Dr. Aybar nonchalantly shrugged off the sloppy loss as opening-game jitters.

By 2:00 p.m. *fanáticos* from both teams were pushing into the stands early to see the two teams warm up for the 3:00 p.m. game. Dr. Aybar took his seat in the front row with other members of the Dragones Board of Directors and the sportswriters.

The Estrellas promptly sent their lineup card onto the field for afternoon game. It read the same as for game one, with the exception of Radames Lopez, who replaced Ruiz at second base.

Soon the field was marked by long afternoon shadows. Going into the seventh, the game knotted up at 4–4. Dr. Aybar relaxed as his Dragones scored runs in the seventh and the eighth, allowing them to enter the bottom of the ninth with a 6–4 lead.[8] Right from the start of the inning, however, things began falling apart. In dramatic fashion the Estrellas rallied for three runs to walk off with a 7–6 victory.

An unholy din of joy echoed in Dr. Aybar's ears as he sat stunned in his seat. After a few minutes he slowly left the stands. Not a word was spoken while the bus was loaded up. The quiet during the long drive back to Ciudad Trujillo was broken only by occasional grunts and mumbles.

This was surely the moment when it began to dawn on Dr. Aybar that his team was in need of a major overhaul. He spent the bus trip home turning over in his head the various ways to improve the Dragones' roster.

Because he had a large hand in writing the rules for the Campeonato por Reelección de Presidente Trujillo, he knew that there were no rules to hinder dropping or adding players on each team's roster; the sole requirement was that the league officials be notified. "Luckily," he must have thought, albeit with some anxiety, "this can be fixed."

The following day the paper of record for Ciudad Trujillo dejectedly reported that the Dragones had "ya al echarse la paloma el primero cargó con la victoria"—as we would say, they had "snatched defeat from the jaws of victory."[9]

9

Royal Prerogative

It wouldn't stop, this rolling rumble boiling up from a brew
of yelling, dancing, whistling, singing:

> I'm coming from the Primavera ballpark
> watching a thrilling game
> in which the arm of the King Bragaña
> making noble and tremendous play
> put down the Escogido.
>
> To the Escogido officials
> only three things will make cry
> the nine zeros by Cocaína
> divine labor by Don Pelayo
> and the extraordinary hitting by Oms.
>
> Run Pilido, look for Dihigo
> to Bejerano, Moncho and Baró
> so they will cry right along with you
> this Escogido defeat
> in the hands of the great champion.
>
> It's a glory for Titico,
> Arango, Funes and Calderón,
> and the Bambino since they could
> beat the team Escogido,
> cry over a thousand times: Licey is the Champ.[1]

"Licey is the Champ . . . Licey is the Champ," they sang over and over in the capital city as the crowd burst out of Primavera ballpark and flooded into El Parque Independencia after the deciding game of the 1929 championship series. The victory marked one of the great comebacks in Dominican baseball history. Their team stood just one game short of elimination. Licey's *fanáticos* were filled with despair. Then, out of the blue, their beloved Tigres came roaring back by ripping off seven straight victories to capture the title and send the capital city into a state of elation.[2]

Hurricane San Zenón flattened Primavera ballpark the following year, so for the next five years fans were able to see only scattered exhibitions. As for 1936? It was a total catastrophe. To their great shame, both capital city teams were forced to withdraw from the national series, as there was no possibility of winning.[3] The nation's fans were stunned that the upstart Estrellas Orientales from the sugar capital took the crown away from the capital city. For the entire off year baseball angst reigned in the capital city.

April 3, 1937: opening day in Ciudad Trujillo, new season, renewed hope for the capital city. Many still slipped and called it Santo Domingo, but they corrected themselves hurriedly, furtively turning their heads slightly while swiveling their eyes to glance over their shoulders to see who might have heard their slip. Because it mattered. It mattered to Trujillo. At first Generalissimo Doctor Rafael Leonidas Trujillo Molina, honorable president of the republic, benefactor of the fatherland, was content collecting titles.[4] As titles alone proved inadequate, he began naming places after himself. He created a Trujillo province and made his birthplace, San Cristóbal, its capital. Next he had the capital city, Santo Domingo, renamed Ciudad Trujillo. Almost as an afterthought the highest mountain was rechristened Pico Trujillo. Nearly every postage stamp issued by the nation that decade bore his image or his family's name.[5]

Chapita of San Cristóbal had become Colonel Trujillo of Santo Domingo. During the summer of 1927, Colonel Trujillo became General Trujillo. One day as General Trujillo made his rounds of government offices in the capital city, he sighted a Spanish beauty who worked as the personal secretary to the executive of the land courts.[6] Discreetly he made inquiries about his "quite white," black-haired Spanish beauty; her name was María Martínez.[7] He learned that in addition to her physical appeal, she had a keen, clever intelligence. And when he looked into her dark, deep eyes, he saw shrewdness not unlike his own.

María's blend of lust and greed, ambition, corruption, and cold-heartedness quickly captured the general's heart. From the start her conservative, middle-class Spanish family was scandalized by her affair with the married general. They promptly asked María to leave the family home.[8] But neither the general nor his mistress was in the least bit troubled. At once he installed her in a nearby furnished apartment. They even conjured up a phony spouse to act as her cover. Within months the general's new bed partner became his business partner. Trujillo handed María the exclusive concession for cleaning and pressing all the uniforms for the Dominican Army. And a very profitable business it was: members of Trujillo's army were required to use María's laundry and charged eight to ten dollars per month even though they pulled down salaries ranging only from fifteen to twenty dollars.[9]

Early one morning in June 1929, an urgent knocking woke the superintendent of a San Isidro sugar plantation, who probably thought it was just another routine annoyance like his field hands having broken another piece of equipment. In a huff he opened his front door. There stood a man from town whom he only vaguely recognized but knew he feared. All at once he remembered that the man was a member of La 42, one of General Trujillo's enforcers. So it was a genuine relief when the man only rudely demanded that his family instantly leave their home—no questions ask.

In minutes the superintendent cleared out his family. The man ordered him to keep people away from the area. Just a few hours later a large car, kicking up a cloud of dust, came barreling down the dirt road to his house. At the door a group of people including a few women got out. It was clear that a fully pregnant woman was the center of all their attention. Later that afternoon the screams of childbirth were heard. The woman's screams subsided and were replaced by the cries of Rafael Leonidas Trujillo Martínez. He would later be called just "Ramfis."[10]

Within a year of Ramfis's out-of-wedlock birth, his father became president. Complicating things was the fact that Bienvenida Ricardo was still Trujillo's wife and first lady, but awkwardly not the mother of the president's son.

Trujillo adored young Ramfis obsessively. When the boy turned three, Trujillo made him a colonel in the army. The following year he named the largest suspension bridge in Latin America after Ramfis. At age five Ramfis celebrated his birthday in public for the first time. Trujillo even ordered the capital-city newspaper to run an item on the party: "Today, the charming and beautiful child, Rafael Leonidas Trujillo Martínez, youngest colonel of our national army, beloved son of Generalissimo Rafael Leonidas Trujillo Molina, honorable president of the republic, reaches and will magnificently celebrate his fifth birthday."[11]

Just a few months later, the same newspaper suddenly reported that the first lady would travel to Europe for a few months on a pleasure trip.[12] While the good wife shopped in Paris, the Dominican Congress got busy passing a law allowing a man to obtain an uncontested divorce if his wife had been unable to bear a child within the first five years of marriage.[13]

It just happened that the first lady had gone well over the five-year limit; she became the first person divorced under the new law.[14] This maneuver proves that a man with an abundance of power and an absence of shame can legally overcome the most challenging of obstacles.

Before 1935 ended, Trujillo married the mother of Ramfis as his third wife. She became Doña María Martínez Alba de Trujillo.[15] But as fate would have it, in the wake of the new marriage, his freshly divorced wife gave birth to a daughter, Odette.[16]

Only a year later, on a clear fall day, as Rafael strolled down the peaceful, shaded, tree-lined streets of the Gazcue district to the west of colonial downtown, a few blocks away from El Malecón, he stopped on his stroll, just to stare. There she stood: a tall, young Spanish-blooded beauty. Her skin was white. Her hair, flowing black, was accented by a high forehead. She looked out at the world through sympathetic almond-shaped eyes. She smiled at it with large pouty lips, ruled by Cupid's bow.

Rafael asked around. She was a Lovatón—daughter of the late distinguished Senator Ramon Lovatón—a name people stopped and took notice of when they heard it. The Lovatóns were among the "best" families; her father had even served as vice president for a short time.[17]

That fall Lina Lovatón happened to be in the thick of the competition to be crowned queen of the upcoming carnival. Trujillo instantly signed up to be her volunteer campaign manager.

So it was no accident, when in the final days of December 1936 Lina was crowned Queen Lina I by the administrative council of Santo Domingo. With urgency a host of events for her coronation were planned: she would be given the keys to the city and issue proclamations naming Trujillo, his wife, and his mother as the "Great and Only Protectors of the Kingdom" and Ramfis her "favorite prince." The following spring Queen Lina I was on hand to bless the dedication of the miniature Washington obelisk at the foot of El Malecón to Trujillo. That night there was an official dance for Queen Lina I at the presidential palace.[18]

• • •

Saturday, April 3, 1937, was opening day for baseball in Ciudad Trujillo in the Campeonato por Reelección de Presidente Trujillo. Of course, Trujillo even saw to it that, "Her graceful Majesty Lina I, queen of the carnival, [would] throw out the first ball of the encounter between the 'Estrellas Oriente' versus 'Ciudad Trujillo B.B.C.'"[19]

After lunch that Saturday *fanáticos* began streaming toward the Campo Deportivo for the 3:00 p.m. game. Many came walking north from the colonial district through the massive clay-colored city gate known as the Puerta de la Misericordia (Gate of Mercy). The fancier set came in cars or horse-drawn carriages from the Gazcue district. Hundreds disembarked along El Malecón off buses and cars arriving from Santiago, San Pedro de Macorís, and other interior cities to watch all three teams in action that weekend.

Shortly after three o'clock Cuban pitcher Rudolfo "Ven por Dios" (Hurry, for God's sake!) Fernández took the mound for the Dragones. Right away the Estrellas scratched out a run against Fernández in the top of the first. Then, with two outs in the second, he walked Estrellas catcher Julio Rojo, bringing Estrellas pitcher Ramon Bragaña to the plate. When the count reached two strikes, Fernández threw a curve. Bragaña hit it deep over the left-field fence onto Calle Piña, where children scrambled for the ball. It was the first home run of the series. He was greeted at home plate by thunderous applause from Estrellas fans who had traveled down the coast to watch their championship team. Estrellas 3, Ciudad Trujillo 0.

Capital-city *fanáticos* grumbled and shifted in their seats when the Estrellas scored yet again to take a 4 to 1 lead in the top of the fifth. Suddenly things fell apart for the visitors. Once the Dragones filled the bases, the cheering turned to a roar that shook the stands. It grew as they scored six runs with a series of walks, bloop hits, and errors to take a 7 to 4 lead.

As it turned out, even though the Dragones notched their first win with a final score of 8–4, the press sounded a sour note of doubt: "The victory of this evening has filled with optimism the local managers." "Serious error," they wrote in *Listín Diario.* Because their team was "inferior to the champions," the victory was merely "many small circumstances, which conspired to produce the defeat of the elephants."[20]

Capital-city fans returned the next day at 3:00 p.m. to cheer on their Dragones in their first game against the newly formed Águilas of Santiago. That day they would be facing American Bert Hunter—at this point the only Negro Leaguer on any of the three teams.

Hunter—the locals called him "King Kong"—dished up his nasty curveball to shut down the Dragones. He started that game by striking out the side in the first. The Águilas scored five runs in the second to put the game out of reach, piling up fourteen hits to win 10 to 3.[21]

It was now clear to the little dentist. For the Dragones to win the Campeonato por Reelección de Presidente Trujillo, he must improve his team's talent. Losing no time Aybar called a meeting of the club's executive committee. It was decided that he should fly off to the United States to hire baseball players from the Negro Leagues—talent like "King Kong" Hunter.

Aybar spent the rest of the week making calls to baseball scouts in America. Toward the end of the week, he packed his bags to catch a plane to Miami. On arrival he picked up a car from the Dominican consulate and drove the eight hundred plus miles to New Orleans.

10

Total Catastrophe

Every afternoon between 1:00 and 3:30, the men sat at long tables with smoke snaking up to the lights from improvised ashtrays. The shades were drawn, with light mostly coming from a cluster of overhead electric bulbs. Their eyes rarely strayed from their stacks of coins and paper except to glance at the ashtray. There was a whirl of activity for the first two hours. Time was beat to the sounds of betting slips flapping as they were sorted and slid under the edges of indexes, coins clinking as they were stacked and counted and the rat-a-tat ching-changing of the adding machines as they were cranked by hand.

Talking came in hushed bursts so as not to break the concentration of the counters and sorters of the policy bank. Everyone stood by as the head banker used the last half-hour to recheck his figures so that he could close his books for the day. Only then could they head to the grill to drink, talk, hear some music, maybe meet a girl who wasn't their wife but didn't care if they had one, knowing that all the bets had been recorded and all the money was ready for deposit at the local bank split up as proceeds from a pool hall, a café, hotels, and a nightclub.

As the men left, they nodded to the jumpy young guard lurking outside the building with his finger near a button, ready to sound a hushed alarm if anyone unfamiliar approached the building out of which Gus Greenlee operated his Pittsburgh numbers racket.[1]

Gus was almost always at the Crawford Grill. He was easy to spot: a large man, with a long, splayed nose; heavy, arching eyebrows; broad, deep eye orbs; a high forehead; and smile lines that acted as a permanent set of parentheses for his friendly mouth. When he wanted something from you that you didn't want to give him, the parentheses disappeared. He got real close to your face so that he could bore into your eyes to make you squirm. But mostly he was charm and laughter.

Gus Greenlee's numbers racket in Pittsburgh's Hill district sold "policies" to his customers. Folks would write down three numbers of their choice. If their lucky three numbers came up, they were paid off at 600 to 1. Even the poorest among the poor seemed to be able to find a penny to buy a "policy," which paid six dollars—half a day's wages for many of those living in the neighborhood.

It was the height of the Depression, and in every urban African American neighborhood in America you could "play the numbers" or "buy a policy." Just like bootlegging, it was an illegal operation that everyone in Pittsburgh, from the police chief to the president of the city council, knew all about but simply looked the other way. Consider the size of Gus's operation: at its height he had a payroll of $1,500 a week in addition to dozens of "runners" all paid on commission. His daily take could be as high as $20,000 to $25,000.[2] It meant he commanded a network so deep in the Hill district of Pittsburgh that on Election Day Gus was able to deploy an army of numbers runners to turn out voters for the politicians of his choice.

• • •

It was the dead of winter 1912 when eighteen-year-old Gus stole away on a freight train heading north out of his hometown of Marion, North Carolina. Folks had told him it would be cold, but he didn't quite understand just how cold until he arrived in Pittsburgh wearing patched pants and white canvas shoes.[3] At first he shined shoes. After a while Gus was able to find a job at a steel mill, where he worked hard to save up enough money to buy a taxicab.

Soon World War I broke out. In no time Private Greenlee was shipped off to France as a member of the Fiftieth Battalion of the 153rd Depot Brigade. When he arrived back in Pittsburgh after the Great War, he found Prohibition in full swing. Gus took his taxi out of mothballs and went back to work. It took him just a few weeks to sniff out something far more profitable than delivering people—that was delivering booze to every corner of the city. Within months Gus had earned the moniker "Gasoline Gus." Before long the gregarious Greenlee had set aside enough money to open a "black and tan" speakeasy in the Hill district where he began booking entertainers for shows. He found he was a natural at this. Before long he opened a booking agency to hire out talent to Pittsburgh's other nightclubs.

Soon Gus's business empire grew to include a pool hall, a nightclub, two hotels, and his new stranglehold on the numbers racket in black Pittsburgh. In a few more years he opened the Crawford Grill and founded the Pittsburgh Crawfords Baseball Club. Standing on Wylee Avenue in Pittsburgh's Hill district, the grill was nearly a full block long with a main hall on the second floor that featured a revolving stage and a glass-topped bar. Gus called the third floor "Club Crawford"; it served as his business headquarters but also as his hangout for friends and VIPs. Before long the Crawford Grill became the cultural mecca of black Pittsburgh; the giants of jazz—Duke Ellington, Count Basie, Cab Calloway, and Louis Armstrong—all played there. Jazz great Lena Horne launched her career at the grill.

Gus founded the Pittsburgh Crawfords baseball team in 1931. He was able to build a strong team quickly by taking advantage of black baseball teams falling on hard times during the Great Depression. So when the Detroit Wolves folded before the 1933 season, he signed the fastest man in baseball, center fielder "Cool Papa" Bell and talented left-hander Leroy Matlock.

Eventually Gus turned to raiding other teams' rosters for talent. He simply took Josh Gibson, Judy Johnson, and Oscar Charleston from the crosstown rival Homestead Grays. It was no accident that by 1933 the best black baseball talent in America played for Gus's Pittsburgh Crawfords. At once they entered into a full-throttled rivalry with the crosstown Homestead Grays that became the talk of black Pittsburgh.

Yet it was Greenlee's signing of the twenty-five-year-old Satchel Paige for $250 a month that made his team the talk of black baseball across America. Satchel had been hidden away pitching in the South and the Midwest. Now pitching for Gus's Pittsburgh Crawfords, Satchel dazzled East Coast fans with his wild array of pitches, windups, and releases—always delivered with pinpoint accuracy. It took no time for the savvy Satchel to figure out his new team owner. Gus "was so sharp," he thought, "that they must have a school for what he would do and he learned real good at that school."[4]

The Crawfords were the class of the Negro Leagues. While most teams drove from game to game in rickety converted school buses and played at small-time fields, the Crawfords rode in a custom-built, freshly painted lime-green Mac bus and played at the newly constructed brick-faced Greenlee Field. The players drew year-round salaries and attended spring training. The Crawfords finished the 1936 season first in the league with a sparkling 42-29 (.589) record. Star slugger Josh Gibson batted .347. Satchel went 6 and 1.

When the baseball season ended, Satchel and his fellow Negro Leaguers made money by barnstorming across America. They played games against town clubs, semiprofessionals, and shtick teams like the Ethiopian Clowns and the House of David. But the most money was always to be had by playing against white Major Leaguers, who like their black counterparts were woefully underpaid. Teams headed by legends roamed the country. Babe Ruth barnstormed. There were Dizzy Dean's All Stars, Bob Feller's All Stars, and many teams of lesser stature. One thing always held true when Satchel and his fellow Negro Leaguers played against white Major Leaguers: they were stunned by the slow pace and conservative style of play. When they heard white managers talk about slow ball as "doing things the right way," they knew it really meant "doing things the white way."

Years later Gene Benson, who played with Satchel against white Major Leaguers, recalled, "We didn't have to worry about gettin' thrown at and knocked on our asses." Benson remembered, "We could stand up and face the pitcher and not have to worry 'bout duckin' and divin'." As for Satchel "he didn't have to worry about them guys up there runnin' all 'round the base paths. He could just go through all the motions he wanted, throw whatever pitch he wanted to, not lay in the fastball. Couldn't have been easier."[5]

It wasn't so in the Negro Leagues. Negro League baseball in the 1930s was fast, brash, and flash. Play featured a combination of speed, aggressiveness, unpredictable bunting, an anytime, anywhere running game, power, bean balls, flamboyance, and a sense of humor. Pitching could mean anything from blazing fastballs, spitballs, shine balls, cut balls, and knock downs— often thrown out of changing, deceptive, intricate windups. You never knew.

Negro League baseball scorned the conservative station-to-station-hit-a-home-run game, which had become the norm in white Major League baseball by the 1930s. There was a flamboyance to boot. Satchel Paige's favorite catcher wore a chest protector emblazoned with the words "thou will not steal." Negro League first baseman Dave "Showboat" Thomas was famous for routinely catching throws at first base behind his back; he especially loved to flash his signature play as a way to put an exclamation mark on an inning-ending double play. Satchel featured a dizzying array of windups and deliveries. His most famous windup was the "hesitation," in which he slowed down but did not stop his motion at critical points to throw off the timing of batters.

Because Negro League and Latin American teams played with small rosters, they were always in need of players who could handle duty at multiple positions. Martín Dihigo was the gold standard. He was a dominant pitcher, sure-handed fielder, and champion hitter. Another famous player, Theodore Roosevelt Radcliffe, was known as "Double Duty" because he often played as catcher and pitcher in back-to-back games.

Most of the Negro Leagues team owners used proceeds from the numbers racket to underwrite their franchises. In addition to the Pittsburgh Crawfords, three other teams were run by numbers men—making it four out of the six teams in the league.[6] As long as Gus Greenlee's numbers racket was solid so were his team's finances.

Come 1936 and 1937 problems began boiling to the surface for Gus as his primary moneymaker began to attract unwelcomed notice. In the summer of 1936, Philadelphia numbers king John "Big Nose" Nazone was standing a few houses down from a corner known as "Bloody Angle" when two men driving by in a small black sedan unloaded a silenced machine gun into him. "Big Nose" fell to the street, hitting his head on the running board of a parked car on the way to the ground. He was rushed to Pennsylvania Hospital, where he died within minutes.[7] It soon became clear to the police that Nazone had been gunned down by the Lanzetti brothers in a dispute over numbers territory.[8] Five months later New York special prosecutor and future presidential candidate Tom Dewey brought the hammer down on Alex "Caliph of Little Harlem" Pompez, owner of the Negro League New York Cubans. Pompez fled Manhattan for Mexico in the wake of Dewey's massive raids on his numbers racket.[9] The feds trailed Pompez all over Mexico in the spring of 1937 but were able to arrest him only after a gunfight near Mexico City.[10]

Unfortunately for Gus all this unwanted attention on the numbers racket unhappily coincided with a run of bad luck for him. "In that year [1937]," one of Greenlee's players would remember, "Gus Greenlee, who was in the numbers racket, had lost a lot of money." Gus had a low-level employee who "was tipping off the detectives whenever they was counting the money." He lost so much money that year that "he was giving the ballplayers a tough way to go."[11]

To right the ship Gus traded his great slugging catcher Josh Gibson and third baseman Judy Johnson, just so he could afford to keep his biggest draw, Satchel Paige.

At first Satchel didn't play along. His opening gambit for upping his 1937 contract was to float a "he'd-like-to-be-traded" item to the black press in January. He had the *Chicago Defender* write: "LeRoy Satchel Paige, greatest living pitcher, perhaps is said to have asked that he be traded or sold to another ball club for the 1937 season."[12] Two months later Satchel was still holding out on Greenlee. The *Pittsburgh Courier* reported, "Satchell Paige, never in a hurry to do anything, is expected to turn in his document late this week, and then motor to Hot Springs [Arkansas] for a little extra conditioning."[13]

Eventually Satchel signed his contract with Gus. Next he drove to Hot Springs for a final tune-up before spring training, but he didn't arrive in New Orleans until early April. Within days of his arrival, Dr. Aybar appeared from the Dominican Republic. After he put out feelers for the whereabouts of the Crawfords, he was able to track down Satchel on a street near his team's hotel in order put a bankbook with $30,000 in it in Satchel's hands.

Gus Greenlee jumped in his car and sped off to New Orleans as soon as he heard of Satchel's defection. Gus hated that Satchel was gone, but he was relieved to learn that Satchel had only taken his friend and pet catcher, Cy Perkins, with him—as far as Gus was concerned no great loss there. Cy was merely a competent journeyman; he was only on Trujillo's payroll to keep Satchel happy.

Hastily Gus ordered his publicist, John Clark, to crank his public relations machine into high gear. Out of spite he was determined to embarrass Satchel, but his chief purpose was to intimidate any of his other players who might be tempted to jump. The headline of the national edition of the *Chicago Defender* screamed "PAIGE JUMPS CRAWFORDS." The *Defender* further announced that Gus had made a "hurried trip to New Orleans to stop the plan, which obviously [would] wreck the Negro national league if allowed to continue."[14]

It didn't take Gus long to pull every political string he could lay his hands on: filing official complaints with the Dominican Republic's ministers in Washington, the State Department, and the Department of Justice; he even went so far as to make a direct complaint to Rafael Trujillo.[15] Gus had the Negro National League issue dire threats to Satchel and all the players jumping to the Dominican Republic. They set May 15 as the deadline for the jumping players to return without consequences.

"These men," Gus proclaimed, "must realize that the league is far larger and more powerful than they are."[16] The league went so far as to threaten the errant players with indictments, which it falsely claimed had "already been issued for all players in the league who ha[d] accepted money from club owners and then left."[17]

At home Gus had public opinion on his side. Even Cum Posey, owner of the rival Homestead Grays, branded Satchel as an ingrate in his weekly newspaper column: "He has been treated royally . . . by Gus Greenlee . . . only to jump to a white club in Bismarck, N.D. in the summer of 1935. He has been publicized to the extreme. . . . Satchell Paige has gotten more out of Negro baseball than anyone ever connected with Negro baseball, Negro baseball does not owe him anything. He owes Negro baseball plenty."[18]

In no time Gus's threats and bellyaching spread the news far and wide that the Dominicans were paying big money for Negro League talent. Suddenly no threat was scary enough to stop the poorly paid Negro Leaguers from jumping to the Dominican Republic. Once Satchel jumped, the New York Cubans lost first baseman "Showboat" Thomas, outfielder Clyde Spearman, and pitcher Taylor. The Black Yankees lost catcher Palm.[19]

What happened next shocked even Gus. Two weeks into the Negro National League season, Greenlee got word that two Dominicans had flown to Pittsburgh to steal more of his players. With ultimate chutzpah Estrellas Orientales president Federico Nina and his friend Luis Mendez approached pitcher "Spoon" Carter at the Crawford Grill and invited him to meet them at a local hotel. Crawfords manager Oscar Charleston flew off the handle and "stormed into the room accusing them of stealing league players who were under contract." Oscar shouted in their faces, "I came here to whip you, but since you're so little I don't do it. Why don't you go into the white leagues and get your players?"[20]

But the ugly confrontation didn't stop the Dominicans. The next day Nina and Mendez had the nerve to buy box seats at Greenlee Field to scout Crawfords players. That was too much. Gus had the Dominicans seized and taken to the office of Alderman Maloney, where they were summarily arrested and thrown into jail. Neither man was able to make the $1,000 bail. The *Pittsburgh Courier*'s headline blared, "TWO JAILED IN BASEBALL WAR—LEAGUE ACTS TO CHECK 'RAIDS.'"[21] The same paper later failed to report that only a few days later both men were released without charges.

As hard as the Negro League owners tried to occupy the high moral ground, the simple truth was they were not paying their star players anywhere near market value. "Hell," Satchel later recalled, "that bunch would hold on to a dollar bill until old George screamed in pain. I mean it. That was one of the tightest bunch of bandits that ever walked; it was like they had fishhooks in their pockets."[22]

The *Chicago Defender* was the only black newspaper that lent a sympathetic voice to Satchel and the jumpers. The *Defender* asked as simple question: Why blame the jumpers? Aren't black players entitled to seek the same salaries as white players? "The mass walk-out on the National Negro League Baseball is reported to have come as a result of low salaries paid. . . . They have no way of getting more than a modest salary. They have no means of becoming nationally famous and capitalizing on their fame as do their white fellow players in the big leagues."[23]

Years later when Satchel told the story of Gus and the jumpers, he would smile and conjure up the movie *Zorba the Greek*. "Remember the movie *Zorba the Greek*, Anthony Quinn plays Zorba," he would laugh, "in the movie whenever things go wrong he says, 'total catastrophe!' And that's what this was, a total catastrophe. Because the minute old Gus opened his big mouth and tried to sue these Cubans everything backfired on him."[24]

Out of the total catastrophe there was one bit of good news for Greenlee's league: the Dominicans had failed to steal Josh Gibson, the "Babe Ruth of the Negro League."

• • •

As Satchel and Cy walked onto the airplane and headed for the Dominican Republic, Satchel nervously queried Aybar to find out if they needed passports for the trip. Flashing a no-worries-just-relax-my-friend smile, the little dentist assured him that everything had been handled. During the winter of 1929–30, Satchel had played in Cuba on the Leopardos de Santa Clara, so he had a feel for the Caribbean flavor of baseball. He wasn't worried about the baseball part of things; it was just like the Negro Leagues—fast, aggressive, and showy.

When the trio reached the Dominican Republic, Satchel and Cy marveled that they "weren't put out no place to let other passengers on. No sir." Satchel recalled, "We had the right of way. And what's more, we didn't even have passports. Not having passports kind of made me uneasy anyway but that president he fixed it up someways."[25]

Aybar dropped off Satchel and Cy at a private club. That night when they walked around the streets for the first time, they loved that even in the best stores, restaurants, or bars there we no signs proclaiming "whites only."

11

The Stars Arrive

They stood. Standing, waiting, waiting, standing in the hot palace office. President Trujillo sat just a few feet away reading through a sheaf of papers, unaware of their presence. The president was dressed in an Irish linen suit with wide lapels. He wore a crisp white shirt adorned with a red and yellow diagonal striped tie. A round gold pin adorned the center of his tie close to the knot. On his left lapel was a gold Dominican shield with the words "Dios, Patria, Libertad" (God, Country, Liberty). There was not a hint of sweat on him. Everything on his desk was so clean and orderly, everything presented like rows of soldiers standing at attention, saluting.

For four minutes Aybar stood with his companions barely moving a muscle. When they began to sweat, the president looked up at them as if previously unaware of their presence. He motioned for them to sit by crinkling his mouth into a slight, inscrutable smile. None of the men dared to take handkerchiefs out of their pockets to wipe the sweat from their brows—it just pooled there.

The president allowed another thirty seconds of silence to loom and settle in the room, knowing that silence was the most potent recipe for discomforting men. He raised his eyes. "As leaders of the Partido Dominicano," he began, "I count on your help with the political and social reconstruction which I am conducting."[1]

The president's gaze fixed on each man, and his eyes bored into them as he fired questions at them about the state of the

Partido Dominicano in each province: How many members? When was your last demonstration of public support? How many citizens attended? What men of stature could they count on to speak at their rallies? How are the churches?

Abruptly the meeting adjourned. While the president had never stated exactly what he wanted the men to do, they knew. For a brief moment they stood in the marble hallway and wiped the sweat from their brows and conferred with one another over how to the split up the tasks for launching the president's 1938 reelection campaign—even though it was two years away.

Within days of the meeting, the capital city newspaper, *Listín Diario*, published a plea signed by all the prominent citizens—it was single spaced and went on for pages—urging Trujillo to run for reelection.[2] Later that summer *Listín* published four single-spaced pages listing Trujillo supporters from Barahona. Everything was building toward a mass event in support of his reelection. It required each party boss to gather citizens from his turf and produce them at a massive fall rally in the capital imploring the president to seek reelection.[3]

As 1936 closed and 1937 loomed, Dr. Aybar together with Trujillo's brother-in-law, Francisco Martínez Alba, again came to see the president. Together they sat in Trujillo's office at the National Palace to bring him up to speed on the progress of his reelection campaign. With great trepidation they proposed an idea, one, they argued, that would be very popular with the common people: a national baseball championship series called Campeonato por Reelección de Presidente Trujillo. They showed their seriousness by telling the president that they were ready to put aside their Licey/Escogido baseball rivalry in order to combine the two capital-city teams into one powerhouse—a team they promised would effortlessly sweep to the championship. Trujillo patronizingly smiled at the men as he listened. He found their passion for baseball silly. But he thought this was smart politics.

Spring unfolded, much baseball was played, but winning this promised baseball championship was not turning out to be as easy as Aybar and Alba had thought or, more urgently, as they had so confidently promised Trujillo. The first sign of trouble came from the Estrellas Orientales of San Pedro de Macorís, the island's sugar capital. It took only a handful of defeats for them to realize that the Estrellas were stocked with talented Cubans and Dominicans and that they would continue to be a tough and annoying opponent. Worse yet the Águilas Cibaeñas from Santiago were quickly becoming a real threat.

• • •

That day everyone in Ciudad Trujillo saw the headline of the sports section in *Listín Diario* about the rival Águilas from Santiago. It read, "EL FAMOSO MARTÍN DIHIGO JUGARA EN EL SANTIAGO" (The Famous Martín Dihigo to Play for Santiago)." "We have reports, on very good authority," the paper confided, "that the 'Santiago Baseball Club' has acquired the services of the famous Cuban baseball player Martín Dihigo y Pinson, a player who is considered the best today throughout Latin America and called with good reason 'Hombre Team.'"[4] "Hombre Team" they called him—"Man Team" or as we might say, "One-Man Team."

Ten days later a throng of *béisbol fanáticos* from Santiago and San Pedro de Macorís gathered to watch a Pan American seaplane from Cuba land at the mouth of the Higuamo River.[5] As the door opened, the crowd spied a dark black man standing six feet three inches, sporting a rock-solid 190 pounds. He ducked his head as he emerged from the seaplane and stepped into the small boat. Here was the player they were all waiting to get a look at: the famous Cuban Don Martín Dihigo y Pinzón, known in his home country simply as El Maestro.

At thirty years old Dihigo was a complete player in the prime of his career. Dominicans knew the magnitude of his talents from his play for the 1929 Escogido team.[6] Although that team had suffered an unprecedented late-season collapse, it was not Dihigo's fault. In fact the team had nose-dived because the directors had failed to sign El Maestro for the entire series, and the team's collapse had happened because Dihigo had been forced to leave early to honor another commitment.[7]

Even at thirty Martín Dihigo had been a professional baseball player nearly half his life; he had made his debut at age sixteen. When Dihigo was just seventeen, he had traveled to the United States to play for Alex Pompez's New York Cuban Stars of the Negro National League. His talent was immediately apparent to all. In no time Dihigo was sought after on the international circuit. Starting at twenty he would begin his year playing winter ball in Cuba, then move on to the American Negro Leagues, and finally play in Venezuela or Puerto Rico.

What first caught the eyes of fans was Dihigo's stunning versatility. He could play any position but catcher, hit for average and with power. Then while playing in the Cuban leagues with the Santa Clara Leopardos in 1935, he established himself as a star pitcher. That year Dihigo posted a 12-4 record while, by the way, leading the Cuban Winter League in batting average (.358), runs (42), hits (63), triples (8), and RBIs (38). The preceding summer in the United States, as player/manager of the New York Cubans, batter Dihigo hit .372 while pitcher Dihigo won seven games against three losses to lead his club to the 1935 Negro National League second-half title.

After gathering his bags from the seaplane, Dihigo and his friends motored along the coast to Ciudad Trujillo, where they stopped for the night. Next morning they left on a four-hour, ninety-five-mile trip cutting across the center of the island to the northern ancient city of Santiago de los Caballeros. As their car headed north, it slowly climbed the rugged road over the eastern edge of the Cordillera Central mountains and down into the El Cibao region. It took a few more hours to reach the city of La Vega, at the northern tip of the Vega Real—a long fertile valley brimming with coffee, cane, tobacco, cacao, maize, and rice. A few miles further they drove through the city of Moca, past the "Bolivia" school where, in the summer of 1899, the dictator Ulises Heureaux had been shot by future president Ramón Cáceres and left on a hot, dusty street to bleed out.

After motoring fifteen further miles down the fertile valley, they reached Santiago, the heart of the Cibao, second city of the Dominican Republic, and the country's breadbasket. Spanish settlers had founded it two years after Columbus arrived in the New World. The city's people were equally proud of the central role that Santiagans had played in the war of independence from Spain.

Dihigo soon discovered that without a doubt the event that was most indelibly seared into the collective memories of Santiagans was the massacre of 1805. It started when after a fierce fight with Dominican troops along the Yaqué River, Santiago fell to the Haitian Army of the North. Haitian general Henri Christophe had occupied the city with his battle-weary troops on what happened to be the Monday of carnival week. Because it was carnival week, the General turned his soldiers loose on Santiago. His soldiers began with rapes. They moved on to looting, torture, and murder. Once Santiagans realized that things had snowballed into an orgy of slaughter, many took refuge in the church. Now that they were surrounded, the soldiers moved in, slaughtered them, and piled their corpses high in the aisles. With the priest still officiating Mass to the corpses, the troops left the church and set it aflame from the outside.

The soldiers left the burning church and spread throughout the city, where they seized little children and bodily tore them to pieces and hacked men and women to death with machetes. A few days later, when the lucky remnant that had fled the massacre returned, they found the naked, rotting, mutilated bodies of the town council strung off the balcony of the Casa

Consistorial. Countless thousands more were killed in other Dominican cities.[8]

Shortly after Dihigo arrived at the Hotel Mercedes on Calle Máximo Gómez, the lights came on in Santiago's square, which was hedged in by government buildings. As dusk took hold, the watchmen began lighting the candles in the lamps of their horse-drawn carriages. Dihigo could hear their clatter and bells as they announced their crossings. He felt the city had an unmistakably Spanish flavor, which reminded him of Habana Vieja in his country's capital. Dihigo wandered down the main street, picked his way through street vendors, was stopped by bootblacks, and walked by drugstores, a big, modern department store, cafés and restaurants, all with people spilling out of them to crowd the sidewalks. Donkeys, cowboys, and spotless automobiles equally occupied the streets.

After a while Dihigo changed into his dinner jacket and made his way up the hotel stairs to the "roof garden." Looking south from the rooftop, he clearly saw the verdant mountains hugged by cumulous clouds and picked out where the Rio Yaqué del Norte emerged from the horizon. In no time Dihigo found the group of men who ran the two-month-old Santiago baseball team, Águilas Cibaeñas, which was one of the three teams vying for the national championship.[9] Together they reviewed all the necessary paperwork to make him an official player. Over fine Cibao cigars and Carlos Primero brandy, they talked over the team's roster, schedule, and most urgently Sunday's game.

On a warm April Sunday morning, Dihigo was driven to El Play Enriquillo, where the Águilas were facing the Estrellas Orientales at 10:00 a.m. and 3:00 p.m. He walked into this simply laid-out stadium, which consisted of two steeply sloped stands with tall sun covers supported by open beams with V-supports near the roofline. These stands met near home plate. Extending from first base and third base were two more, only slightly sloped stands, which extended along the foul lines by the outfield. The fans in these seats were shaded from the sun by smaller exposed covers.

Dihigo's spirits lifted when heard a local orchestra playing as the fans filtered in and the teams warmed up. The locals told him the orchestra was called Lira del Yaqué, and it stayed during the game to play between innings. During the seventh-inning stretch, Dihigo smiled when the orchestra played its signature merengue, "Compadre Pedro Juan" by Luis Alberti:[10]

Compadre Pedro Juan baile el jaleo
Compadre Pedro Juan que esta sabroso
Aquella niña de los ojos negros que tiene el
Cuerpo flexible baila en empaliza

[Friend Pedro Juan dance the *jaleo*
Friend Pedro Juan it is lovely
That girl with the black eyes has a
Supple body and dances close to her]

Compadre Pedro Juan no pierda el tiempo
Compadre Pedro Juan saque su dama
Se acabara el merengue y si no anda con cuidao
Se quedara como perico atrapao

[Friend Pedro Juan don't waste time
Friend Pedro Juan ask your girl
The merengue will soon end so don't be cautious or
You'll be left behind like a trapped lovebird]

The hometown Águilas split the two games with the visiting Estrellas—dropping the morning one by a score of 2 to 1. They came back to win the late afternoon game, which featured a sensational triple play turned by the Águilas in the fifth inning, with a score of 3 to 1. In the late game Dihigo made his pitching debut as a reliever. Next morning the newspaper called his performance "brillante."[11]

Signs of change began to appear when a small notice ran in the capital-city newspaper on April 10 reporting that Francisco Martínez Alba had been appointed assistant manager of the Dragones.[12] But *Listín*'s readers were as yet unaware that the real moves were being made out of sight by Dr. Aybar, who had traveled to New Orleans. Now stagnant at .500, the Dragones had fallen behind the Estrellas, who were playing at a .666 clip. Even worse than its mediocre record, this team's talent was clearly inferior to the competition. With each passing game Aybar grew sicker knowing that his Dragones were at best a flip of the coin to win any given game.

"LOS PLAYERS PERKING Y PEIZ, LLEGARON POR AVIÓN EL DOMINGO 18," read the headline. Aybar had called the story into the *Listín Diario* copydesk, which had butchered the spellings. By Perking the paper meant Perkins and by Peiz, Paige; the paper reported that they were arriving by airplane on Sunday April 18.[13]

Satchel and Cy glued their faces to the tiny window to see exactly how this plane was going to land on water. They laughed as they watched water shoot up in high arcs trailing the plane as it skidded to a stop on the surface of the Higuamo River. A boat came to pull their plane alongside the pier at San Pedro de Macorís. Once they had gathered their bags, the group walked to the threshold of the pier, where they hopped into a car that Aybar had waiting for them.

First the trio stopped for a late lunch in the downtown. Around 4:00 p.m. they rode out to Tetelo Vargas Stadium to catch the end of the second game between the Santiago Águilas and the San Pedro de Macorís Estrellas. It was the middle of the fifth when they arrived; the score stood Estrellas 1, Águilas 0. Word of the new players presence spread rapidly through the stands. All heads craned to catch a glimpse of the famous Satchel Paige. Satchel, Cy, and Aybar watched the Estrellas bat in the bottom of the fifth. Rojo popped out to first. Bragaña singled to deep short. Ruiz flied out to center. Tetelo hit a routine grounder to third. Thankfully for the third baseman, he could throw to second for the force instead of trying to make a play on the speedy Tetelo at first.[14] Satchel and Cy must have shaken their heads in disbelief at Tetelo's speed—he was the only player they had ever seen who rivaled Cool Papa Bell.

With the windows of their Packard rolled down, the trio sped west down the Caribbean coast through the tropical twilight past endless fields of sugarcane blowing rhythmically in the breeze. Tall cumulus clouds sat over the hills to the north. Turquoise, yes, the water looked turquoise in spots.

Aybar must never have stopped talking, without doubt chatting nonstop about the accommodations President Trujillo was providing for his players. Aybar's sentences surely ran into paragraphs and then into pages so seamlessly that it seemed as if the man didn't breathe while he talked. Satchel could only have smiled, glanced out the window, and hit his internal mute button to tune out the good doctor.

Finally, they neared the capital city. Patches of palms and tiny farms replaced the fields of cane. Coming into view was a white bridge and an old Spanish fort rimmed with medieval turrets. Finally they crossed the Ozama River, and Aybar must have turned tour guide, pointing out the very spot where Christopher Columbus had moored his boats—in fact the very tree, which after all these centuries was still standing, to which the great navigator had tied his boat in the year 1496.

As it grew dark, Aybar pulled his car up to a fine-looking club and showed them to their rooms. Once they put down their bags, he took them down the hall and knocked on a door. Opening the door with a smile was their friend Jabbo. You couldn't blame him for using only his nickname; his parents had named him Herman-Herman Andrews. Aybar politely introduced them all and left. They knew Jabbo well having played with him on the 1932 Pittsburgh Crawfords. At six feet three he was as tall as Satchel but well filled out at 190 pounds. Jabbo hadn't jumped from the Negro Leagues; he had been recruited to play for the Dragones after he finished playing the Cuban Winter League for the Havana Reds. With his powerful lefty bat, he had led that league in home runs.

Satchel and Cy unpacked their suitcases, put on their best night-on-the-town clothes, and fetched Jabbo to hit the town.

It was a warm night in Ciudad Trujillo. When the ocean breeze blew, it felt like Mobile, Alabama. Satchel wore his double-breasted square square patterned blazer with a white pocket square, matching ivy cap, white shirt, red tie, and white linen slacks.

As the three ambled down Calle Archbishop Nouel, they felt like they were in the American South: people were gathered outside their homes just sitting on chairs, watching, laughing, drinking, chatting, joking, arguing, playing cards. All the stucco-faced homes had their windows open. Through the windows flowed the sounds of Spanish singing from radios, dinner conversations, the play of children. Satchel and Cy were amazed to see folks white, black, and everything in between all thrown together, like nothing.

Jabbo took them to Café Lindbergh, where they ordered empanadas of crab and conch, stewed, sweet orange peels, rice, and beer. Over dinner he gave them the rundown: No games until next Saturday, no practice until 2:30 next day. The coaches were pushovers. Everything was within walking distance: stadium, restaurants, stores, bars—hell, even the brothels, which the locals called *casas de chicas*.

After the trio finished their dinner, they wandered down to Calle El Conde. No problem in Ciudad Trujillo finding the right neighborhood or the right street or the right restaurant or the right bar for "coloreds"—hell, everyone down here seemed like they had some color.

They headed to a nightclub that Jabbo knew about. It was loud with chatter mixed with the sound of merengues. Couples danced with a seriousness of purpose, but still they managed to relax and laugh. Satchel, Cy, and Jabbo sat, drank, danced. Danced, drank, sat. Drank, sat, danced.

Finally they headed out to a *casa de chicas*. Jabbo knew where that was too.

Next day, they peeled themselves out of bed. They took little notice that it was closer to lunch than breakfast. They walked downstairs to find a full spread of coffee, melon, pineapple, toast, and eggs. At 2:00 p.m. they gathered up their gear to head over to the ballpark.[15]

Word of Satchel and Cy's arrival quickly spread through Ciudad Trujillo. "The enthusiasm is overflowing," *Listín Diario* reported. "The bets abound. You hear the public clamor— they are burning with desire for the games to begin." Satchel and Cy had instantly become "the topics of most heated comments and conversations of street ballplayers, on squares, corners, and sports gatherings."[16]

At 2:30 that Monday afternoon a huge crowd assembled at the Campo Deportivo to catch a glimpse of Satchel and Cy as they participated in their first team practice. Always the showman Satchel worked through his routine with flair: he fielded bunts, hit balls to the infield, chased flies, worked out at third. When he was sweating, he started to throw. The sound of his fastballs popping in Cy's glove echoed off the walls of the stadium. "Bolas relámpagos," "lightening balls," the *fanáticos* kept saying. They shook their heads in disbelief.[17]

As the weekend approached, a large item ran in the newspaper promoting the weekend games: "Sensational debut," it promised, "of the colossal pitcher Paige and catcher Perkins." "Do not miss these encounters," it gushed, "which will be of real emotional impact."[18]

12

Después de la Victoria

It was a magnificent, sunny April afternoon ... *ululaba*
cheers in the stands and throughout the GRANDSTAND, a perfect
picture of a cosmopolitan audience, cheering for the same
exciting event with a vertigo of fever and madness ... the heavy
atmosphere of cigar smoke. We were all agog with pounding
anxiety. It was a unique feeling in the stands ... very different
from public theaters and rides. In the streets the air of the dry
afternoon was torn by the sour howls of the horns. Under
the rare splendor of the golden sun ... passed buses filled with
a bustling public that overflowed the platforms and countless
cars. They came to witness the fair, elegant people—the victors
of life—artists ... bankers ... politicians. ... It was a human river
that overflowed into the streets through which flowed the stream
of life. ... The public roared in the bleachers and showed their
impatience waiting for the long-awaited "Play ball" to be called
by the umpire. ... Meanwhile the silhouette of the *Memphis* is
lost in the blue abyss ... as a monument to short-sightedness
still ... without soul ... without movement. ... What was a
battleship of immense power is now in continuous sleep,
lulled under the ancient song of the sea.

—PARA GUIGÓ, announcer, Radio Station HIZ

It was a sight that caught them by surprise. Standing at home
plate Satchel and Cy looked out over the right-field fence,

past the palms, into the Caribbean. There it sat: a blend of gray, black, and rust, a five-hundred-foot denuded warship, solid as a rock on the rocks. Its sheer bulk was swelled by four giant smokestacks overtopped by a conning tower. An odd effect was created by waves crashing over the deck and rhythmically spilling down the island side like a waterfall facing the stadium.

The mystery was easily solved. Satchel and Cy were told that this was the carcass of the USS *Memphis*, which had carried an invading force of U.S. Marines to the island in 1916. It had sat there now for over twenty years from the day on which forty men had died as it was battered into silence and left grounded by seventy-five-feet-high rogue waves.

Since the news of Satchel's and Cy's arrival, tickets for the Sunday games had been selling briskly at Café Hollywood on Calle El Conde, even though the prices had been raised. In current U.S. currency values, preferred numbered seats now sold for two dollars, upper stands eighty cents, low bleachers fifty cents, children upstairs forty cents, children downstairs twenty-five cents, *sol* (sunned bleachers) thirty cents, and *campos* (grass) twenty cents.[1]

Early Sunday morning when Satchel glanced out the window of his room, he was astonished to see that the city was already abuzz. He soon discovered the reason when he reached the street: Ciudad Trujillo had awakened at 6:30 a.m. for the lottery drawings. Satchel and Cy joined up with Jabbo to walk to the stadium. It too was buzzing. The scene at the entrance gates was sheer chaos. Buses were unloading, cars were fighting for space with horse-drawn carriages, and vendors were hawking everything from seat cushions to programs to fried plantains. Many more *fanáticos* came streaming to the doors on foot from the north and east. They squeezed into the ticket lines for entrance only to then join the game of jostling for good seats.

Satchel, already warmed up from his hot bath, never stopped moving, batting, fielding, running, bunting, and throwing to Cy. Today the Dragones would play two games against the national champion Estrellas Orientales, who came into the game with a 6-3 record. At 3-3 the Dragones were treading water.[2]

The Estrellas' lineup had not changed since March; Cubans and Dominicans dominated it. Now newly stocked with imports from the American Negro Leagues, the Dragones fielded a fresh lineup featuring pitcher Satchel Paige, catcher Cy Perkins, and outfielder Herman Andrews.

The crew chief shouted for the game to begin that Sunday at 9:30 a.m. sharp. Satchel slowly walked to the mound to the accompaniment of a swelling din with a style that said, "I know I am the center of attention—and I'm well worth it—so pay attention 'cause I will make things happen." For the first three innings, the *fanáticos* were convinced as Satchel effortlessly cut through the Estrellas lineup. His team scored a single run for him in the top of the fourth. Suddenly the wheels came off. Satchel became uncharacteristically wild, yielding three runs in the bottom of the fourth. Then he coughed up three more in the bottom of the fifth, which forced the manager to pull Satchel and replace him with Fernandez. The game went into extra innings tied 7-7.[3] Luckily for Satchel the Dragones pushed across a run in the bottom of the eleventh to win in dramatic fashion. The Dragones took the 3:00 p.m. game by a score of 5-3.

On Monday morning, the headline of *Listín Diario* read: "EN DOS REÑIDOS ENCUENTRO EL 'CIUDAD TRUJILLO BASE BALL CLUB' ESCALA EL PRIMER PUESTO DEL CAMPEONATO AL VENCER A LAS 'ESTRELLAS ORIENTALES'" (After two tight encounters the Ciudad Trujillo Baseball Team vaults into first place of the championship series after beating the Estrellas Orientales). Two victories. First place. Yet the writers and *fanáticos* of the capital city remained unconvinced. In fact, they found things downright disconcerting. The Monday edition of *Listín* branded Satchel's first start in the sub headline as *pobre* (poor). After all he had yielded six runs in five innings.[4]

On Wednesday a column appeared in the paper, pseudonymously signed "Capitaleño." Its headline read: "DESPUÉS DE LA VICTORIA" (After the victory). "Sad for those who rest on their laurels!" Capitaleño began. For "one must note coolly the reality that there are flaws, and we should try to correct them." These last two victories, Capitaleño declared, should have been won by wider margins. Instead they were decided by "fate." Paige's pitching was skewered as "wild" and "ineffective." Perhaps, Capitaleño guessed, this could have been because of "lack of training." Or maybe it was the "abrupt climate change" or even, "excesses taken last week" or "any other cause."[5]

Capitaleño prescribed a severe clampdown on the players. The Dragones must implement "urgent regulations to control the behavior of the players." And these "urgent regulations" must be imposed "without weaknesses of any kind." Capitaleño went on to advocate that the Dragones improve their talent by adding two more players: "one infielder who is a good bat for the middle of the lineup ... the other a pitcher (preferably left handed)."[6]

Then he delivered the kicker. In an isn't-it-obvious-to-everyone tone, he ominously reminded his readers that this wasn't just about baseball. Rather, he wrote, the "honor of the Capital is committed to this great sports tournament and the team must uphold the prestige of the glorious name that it holds—the name alone is a symbol of victory and of the dignity of the flag." In other words the stakes of this series were considerably higher than mere sports—the prestige of the name Trujillo was at risk.[7]

Satchel and his friends were blissfully unaware of the content of the local newspapers. As players used to playing every day, they loved the lazy rhythm of this island baseball series: No more than three games a week, with the games only on the weekends. Practices fell in the afternoons. And aside from the weekends, they could sleep late, laze around in morning, and play at night.

The writers and *fanáticos* loved the rhythm as well: baseball, lottery, and parties on the weekend; sit back and enjoy the gossip and tidbits of news about the three teams during the week. It made things even better that everyone had open rosters. Each week the *fanáticos* watched with great anticipation for the teams to sign new star players.

The day before the "DESPUÉS DE LA VICTORIA" headline appeared, the steamship *Coamo* arrived in Trujillo's new port. On board were Negro League outfielder "Big Splo" Spearman and catcher "Spoony" Palm. Dihigo had telegraphed them and lured them into playing for the Águilas.[8]

Friday of the same week brought news about a complaint lodged by Estrellas catcher and manager Julio Rojo against Trujillo's Dragones. Rojo charged that the Dragones had not properly enrolled Satchel and Cy on the team's roster. It was duly reported that the National Baseball Jury had rejected the Estrellas' complaint as "misguided."[9]

Next a searingly racist piece by Siul, a sportswriter, landed in the Saturday paper. "The legendary Paige," he wrote, "proved to be a myth—he was chased in five innings, in which hitting was rampant." Siul called the three Negro Leaguers "a very important trilogy of monkeys." He riffed on the popular image of the "see no evil, hear no evil, speak no evil monkeys," suggesting that Paige, Andrews, and Perkins "see, hear, and shut up."[10]

The Dragones' next game was scheduled for Saturday at 3:00 p.m. They would be playing the Estrellas at the Campos Deportivo Municipal. From what they knew, the *fanáticos* had every reason to feel optimistic: they had star players from the United States, their team was in first place, and it was the first day of May. Their hopes were quickly dashed: the Estrellas scored seven runs in the top of the third with a fusillade of hits off Fernández. Even the 12–7 final score was misleading, as the game was never close. Satchel did not pitch. Cy went o for 4 with 2 errors. Even Andrews was pulled from right field and replaced by Castaños after going o for 2.[11]

Later that night a dejected Dragones team packed onto the team bus to make the long drive over the mountains to Santiago. They arrived late at their hotel. Next morning at 9:00 a.m. sharp, Dihigo took the mound for the Águilas. He quickly posted a zero. Satchel matched Dihigo's zero. The teams remained locked in a scoreless tie until Dihigo homered off Paige with one on in the bottom of the third. Turning the tables on Dihigo in the top of the fifth, Satchel tied the game at 3–3 with a double. But in the seventh and eighth innings, the Águilas scratched out single runs to win 5–3.[12]

The 3:00 p.m. game was even tighter. Three Águilas pitchers—American right-hander Bert "Buffalo" Hunter, Cuban left-hander Luis "Sir Skinny" Tiant, and Dihigo—held the Dragones to two runs to prevail 3–2 in eleven innings.[13]

It quickly got grim. Monday morning's headline in *Listín Diario*'s sports section screamed across the entire page, "'CIUDAD TRUJILLO' LOSES THREE GAMES IN THE STANDINGS, YIELDING FIRST PLACE TO THE 'ESTRELLAS,' AND SECOND TO THE 'ÁGUILAS CIBAEÑAS.'"[14]

The standings now read:

	Won	Lost
Estrellas Orientales	5	3
Águilas Cibaeñas	5	5
Ciudad Trujillo Dragones	5	6

The only saving grace was a commentary piece by Siul. The same man who had called Satchel a monkey in a previous column singled him out for praise in his subheadline: "Good outing for Paige."[15]

After arriving late Sunday night from Santiago, Paige and

his friends headed out for "a helluva time" on the town. There were no "whites only" signs in Ciudad Trujillo, nothing but green lights. They enjoyed open season on "rum and the senoritas and the mariachis," all the while knowing they could sleep in as long as they wanted Monday morning because team practice wasn't until late that afternoon and the next game ... well, that wasn't until next Sunday morning.[16]

13

Nuevos Rumbos

It was too much. It was time.

It took the better part of an hour for the men to gather on this hot day. They must have formed in clumps under the speckled shade of the park's trees and smoked. Waited. Spit. Grumbled. All heads turned as a man with a high forehead, deep-set eyes, and raven-black hair walked onto the scene. They were given instructions to scare but not harm.

With that the men instinctively formed into a semi-column and rhythmically marched past storefronts and vendors along the streets of the capital city's commercial district. When they arrived at the offices of newspaper *Listín Diario*, they calmly filed in. In sync they spread out, taking positions in every department. Two men stood guard over each entrance.

Trujillo's gang-member friend, Miguel Ángel Paulino, walked up to the publisher and threatened him in no uncertain terms. The publisher was too shaken to say anything. His paper had written about the violence that Paulino's gang had inflicted on the country during the May elections. All he could do was vaguely gaze around and shake his head, as if in agreement. And then, after a few long moments, Paulino and his men left.

Paulino's message was received but not heeded. The next day *Listín's* publisher ran a story on the storming of its offices by Trujillo's men.[1]

Immediately *Listín's* government printing contracts were canceled. When this measure didn't work, Trujillo had publisher Arturo Pellerano Sarda thrown in prison. No one knew exactly what happened there. But when Pellerano was released, *Listín* announced that the paper would be spearheading Trujillo's 1934 reelection campaign.[2]

From that day on *Listín* became the central forum for Trujillo's public denunciations of government officials and citizens. A pattern came to be predictable. One day a seemingly small, critical item would run. It would mushroom into a bigger story. Public outcry would follow, then official action. A career might be wrecked. A man might stand trial, go to prison, or even die. Few things struck more fear into the hearts of Dominicans than reading a small item about their misdeeds in the pages of *Listín* because everyone knew these items were penned by Trujillo himself or at his command by one of his lieutenants.

• • •

People awoke the next morning in Ciudad Trujillo to a cutting story. "There needs to be energy," the paper read, "in the running of the Ciudad Trujillo Baseball Club." The news appeared in the form of an open letter to "Doctor José Enrique Aybar, Deputy to the National Congress and Vice President of the Ciudad Trujillo Baseball Club."[3]

It began ever so politely:

> It has never been considered a good system to criticize the work of baseball managers, as we know how difficult it is to agree with fans, many of whom understand absolutely nothing of the strategies necessary and appropriate in a game-tactics and other resources that managers make use of in certain cases to solve difficult situations for their teams.
>
> We will not therefore criticize this work. We're talking about another kind of leadership. We refer to the lack of energy in the Directorship of the Ciudad Trujillo Baseball Club.[4]

Then it turned to the central point: the "licentiousness" of the foreign players, "whose lavish salaries led to such luxury and allow[ed] all kinds of excesses," was wrecking the Dragones.[5]

The indictment of Satchel and his friends was public, point-by-point, and stark: Night after night Satchel and his friends were "going from one place to another drinking and partying, throwing around money," drinking "until they [fell] down." "They spen[t] nights in the brothel because they" had no "threat of a fine." They were "simply going through the motions with their training, not do[ing] real training." They went to practices "at two-thirty in the afternoon and by four abandon[ed] it to prepare for their nocturnal activities." They were plain spoiled, like members of the bourgeoisie; "naturally they practice[d] tired, listless—not like athletes whose muscles vibrate in the heat of exercise but as bourgeoisie spoiled from a long nap, after the usual helping of rich dishes." They were simply out of control; "nobody control[ed] this group." Worst of all, notwithstanding their bad behavior, these foreign players had "not seen more than loving pampering from the senior coaches of the 'Ciudad Trujillo' Baseball Club."[6]

The poisonous letter was signed by the sportswriter Ismael Mendez, who went by the pseudonym "TOROMBOLO," but it was undoubtedly written by Aybar himself.

It was clear that Satchel and his friends had quickly figured out that Trujillo "ran the place." But they had no idea about the true extent of that "running." Prostitution? Trujillo's brother Romeo "Pipi" Trujillo ran that.[7] Gambling? Brother Romeo again. Hotels, bars, and restaurants? They all reported to the *policía*. And the *policía*? Trujillo ran that too.

The day of the open letter, Satchel's team played the Águilas at the Campo Deportivo, and Satchel had his best outing yet. He yielded five runs on six hits in pitching his team to an 8–5 victory. The only real blemish on his day was a two-run homer belted by Dihigo in the top of the sixth.[8]

Sunday was another matter altogether. That day the Dragones traveled down the coast to San Pedro de Macorís, where they dropped two games to the Estrellas—this time by scores of 8 to 1 and 6 to 2.[9] Monday morning found the Dragones in last place.

Suddenly everything changed. With the weekend games, which marked the midpoint of May, a shake-up was announced. José Sabino resigned as manager, the story politely explained, for "not being able to attend to his duties, given his many occupations." Of course he had been fired. Hostos Fiallo, former manager of the Escogido Lions, took his place.[10]

Manager Fiallo's first game was a success. Satchel turned in his best pitching performance to date, posting a tight 4–3 victory over the Águilas at the Campo Deportivo. The press expressed its admiration: "Satchel Paige, the magnificent pitcher of color, yesterday showed his value after holding the Cibao machine of destruction to four hits."[11] The new manager, however, dropped his second game by a score of 6–2 to the Águilas, and Monday again found the Dragones in last place in the standings. Satchel's record, however, was finally a respectable 2-1.

Midweek the next shoe dropped. It started with a small item in Wednesday's edition of *Listín Diario* announcing that a new executive committee, headed by Dr. José Enrique Aybar, had been formed to put the team back on track. But *Listín* had buried the lead: A committee called "Encargados de la Disciplina y Organización" (Managers of Team Discipline and Organization) had been formed. Among its members was Trujillo's gang-member friend, Miguel Ángel Paulino.[12]

The final shoe dropped on Saturday morning under *Listín Diario*'s headline "NUEVOS RUMBOS ORIENTAN AL CIUDAD TRUJILLO BASE BALL C" (New directions for the Ciudad Trujillo Baseball Club). The article that followed made public the full extent of the shake-up. The "new managing director for the stretch run," it reported, would be Dr. José Enrique Aybar, "a man of action, dynamism, clear thought, and of real weight."[13]

More good news: The new committee had announced that it had just signed four additional Negro League stars, Harry Williams, Leroy Madlock, James "Cool Papa" Bell, and Sammy Bankhead. The four had left Wednesday night on a train from Pittsburgh to Miami, where a plane sent by the new committee had picked them up. They were scheduled to arrive that Saturday night to make their debut with the Dragones.

Then the hammer fell. The article reported that the four new players were "stars of the first magnitude," and everyone would now be subject to "mas estricto control" (the strictest control).[14]

Mas estricto control. For that there was Trujillo's friend Miguel Ángel Paulino. He was put in charge of the *estricto control* part of the "Nuevos Rumbos." *Listín Diario* reported that Paulino had been "entrusted with the organization and discipline of the team." Leaving no doubts the newspaper noted that Paulino's appointment represented an "absolute guarantee of the honest and tidy life the new players [had] to live in the capital city for the Ciudad Trujillo Baseball Club."[15]

That afternoon at the Campo Deportivo, Satchel threw his best game yet of the series. He beat the Estrellas 4–1, yielding just six hits, while striking out five and walking only three batters. The Dragones third baseman, Silvio García, was the offensive star of the game, connecting on two key hits, one of them a double, while scoring two runs.[16]

After the game the Dragones made the long trek over the mountains to Santiago. In the morning game Dihigo shut them out 5–0. Mercifully they were rained out for their afternoon game.[17] The weekend left the Dragones stranded in last place— with the quiet, positive notes being that Paige was now at 3–1, and the Estrellas had fallen into second place.

Señor Paulino's Guards of Team Discipline and Organization Committee quickly kicked into high gear. Monday the new regime of *mas estricto control* was in full swing.

Wherever Satchel and his friends went, Paulino's men went.

And it didn't matter how innocuous the activity; as Satchel recalled, "No matter what we did—like if we went swimming—there were soldiers around."[18] Trips to the Calle El Conde were still fine—with the soldiers. Restaurants for dinner were still fine—with the soldiers.

Bars and nightclubs were not so fine. Trujillo had put out the word. From that moment on Satchel and his fellow American ballplayers found it impossible to get a drink; as Satchel later explained, "The president he gave an order that none of the American ballplayers could be sold whiskey. And we weren't either. The guy that done it would have been shot."[19] The same rules applied for the various other activities the ballplayers enjoyed; nightclubs, *casa de chicas—mas estricto control*.

No matter what Satchel and his friends did, no matter where or when, there were Paulino's men. Paulino's men even made sure the players were "in bed early."[20] Paulino's soldiers worked in shifts, so they could keep tabs on the players all night long.[21] "It was almost," Paige mused, "like we were in jail."[22]

14

Black Babe Ruth

It was still dark, before dawn. Hattie walked slightly behind him to the front door where his bags were laid out. There wasn't much—a long canvas sports bag with bats, mitts, and catcher's gear—a smaller canvas bag with his shaving kit, toothbrush, and clothes. She had discovered how heavy those bags were the night before when she moved them a few feet to clear a better path to the door. Yet the next morning he picked them up with his broad, muscled shoulders as if they were weightless.

It was only a ten-minute drive to the Pittsburgh train station, which stood beside the Monongahela River, a handful of blocks from where it flowed into the Allegheny. After only a few minutes, Hattie and Josh could see the five-story, red-brick train station rising above its neighbors. Its chimneys tapered outward as they rose like candelabras, granite archways framed the entrances, and lightning rods topped its steep gray-green roof. On this warm June Tuesday, the station was already thronged with travelers arriving in taxis and private automobiles.

Josh kissed Hattie good-bye with a distance she accepted as all he had to offer. When he stepped out of the car with his two bags, the black redcap smiled, widening his eyes in recognition.

The stationmaster announced in a loud, singsong voice: "Capitol Limited for McKeesport, Connellsville, Cumberland, Martinsburg, Washington, Baltimore, Wilmington, Chester, Philadelphia, Wayne Junction, Jersey City, Brooklyn and New York leaving on track number 3." Half a minute later, a tenor voice cut through all the other sounds, "Aaaalllll-aborrrd." Soon came the sixteenth-note clanging of the bells in G. Josh quietly took his seat on the train. He scanned the faces of his fellow passengers, all white. Not one of them knew who he was.

Soon the train had left the city and was traveling into the Alleghenies, spotted with ash, spruce, and fir. As his body relaxed to the rhythm of the train, his mind was absorbed by the moving scenery. The decisions of the past few months flowed through him. Satchel always followed a dollar bill—heck, someday he'd probably follow a dollar bill right over a cliff. When Satchel smelled money he just plain took off, almost didn't matter where. Once he'd taken off for Bismarck, North Dakota. Even lived in an old train car there 'cause white people wouldn't rent to him. Janet wasn't so happy about that one. But in that town there was a rich guy who owned a Chrysler dealership, and he paid Satchel plenty—even gave him a new car when he had won him enough games. Almost gave Gus Greenlee a stroke that time when Satchel up and left him high and dry in New Orleans and flew off to the islands to play ball. Gus was getting everyone involved in that one, even Washington DC, wasn't doing him much good, just kicking up a lot of dust. Josh had never liked the way Satchel did things, had never done things his way. Sure enough those boys from the islands had come to him with a real good deal, but he had talked it over with Cum Posey. He didn't up and run away. Just laid it all out man to man. Cum wasn't real happy or anything, but he let Josh know that he thought a baseball player needed to make what he could when he could. And because he couldn't come close to that, he just let Josh go—and told him to come on back in July when he was done.

The air had gotten hot, sticky, and heavy by the time the train arrived at Washington's Union Station after midday. Once Josh retrieved his bags, he searched for the Florida Special platform. He remembered that he not only needed to find the right platform; he also needed to find the right section of the right platform, the colored section. From here all the way to Miami, he would need to travel in the colored car, which always stood near the front of the train, just behind the locomotive and baggage car—right near all the noise, smoke, and cinders.

Josh stood on the platform among the other black passengers and could feel that they were all pretending not to look at him while looking at him. He saw their lips move as they semi-whispered his name, "There's Josh Gibson, the famous baseball player." When he boarded, his fellow passengers insisted he take a seat near the back. As nice as that was, it didn't do much good. Even though it was plenty hot inside, they had to keep the windows in the rickety wooden colored car closed; otherwise the cinders and the smoke from the locomotive would pour right in.

The sweat soaked clear through Josh's clean white shirt in no time. As the train ran through Virginia, his mind would have filled with pictures of his childhood, especially that summer chasing baby Jerry all over the farm. There was just about nothing that his baby brother didn't try to eat. You name it: pine needles, bark, dirt, donkey poo. He thought it was all a big, fun game. The only thing to do was to carry him down to the creek, wash him all out, starting with his mouth, and get him chasing the chickens or riding the dogs. Boy, did those dogs and chickens run when they saw baby Jerry coming. Didn't matter how hard a day Mom had in the fields with Dad, she always had dinner on the table for the family. Cooked in the black-and-white spattered pots over a fire she'd started with a lighter knot—nothing was better than a fresh chicken, corn, and purple string beans out of her dinner pot. Mom canned everything you might ever think about eating: sausage, peaches, baked beans, asparagus, ham, pears, peas, corn, spinach, chicken, okra, and carrots. She kept them safe and cool in a cellar Dad had dug under the floorboards of the house. She must've had hundreds of things down there; Mom knew down to the jar everything she had put up. She also had just about every kind of root you could ever imagine. And if anything went missing, she knew that too, and you had better watch out then because she'd sure get to the bottom of it and there'd be hell to pay.

On Sundays they all dressed up and went to the white-painted church, where they heard the minister preach in his low-pitched, smooth, but loud voice. They would all sing:

Joshua fit de battle ob Jericho, Jericho, Jericho
Joshua fit de battle ob Jericho
An' de walls come tumblin' down

He was named after Joshua. Dad had said that Grandpa was named after Joshua, and he was named after Grandpa, who had been a slave living just down the road when he was freed by Abraham Lincoln.

One day Dad got to talking to Mom. Afterward she said he was going away for a while, but he would send the family money. One day he came back, dressed all fancy, and told them about the smoky city with the steel mills. Not too long after that baby Annie came. Not much later he sent for the family to come north. They took everything they could carry and got on the train at the small platform in Buena Vista, Georgia. Mom had packed food for them, which they needed because the trip took days. The cities got bigger and bigger until they finally came to the biggest one of all. That day Dad, dressed up in nice shoes and a hat, came from the steel mill and took them from the train station to a real brick house that was really theirs at 2410 Strauss Street, Pleasant Valley.

As the train steamed through Georgia, talk in the colored car turned to Willie Reed, the young man from Bainbridge recently arrested for murdering a white man. The passengers recounted how the sheriff, who claimed that Reed was trying to run away, had shot him in Albany. Willie's family took him to the undertaker to bury him, but that night a mob of white people from town broke in, stole his body, and tied the corpse to the back of a car. They drove around and around the town square, dragging Willie's lifeless body while a large crowd hooted and hollered. Once the mob grew tired of dragging the corpse, they took Willie's body out to the Negro baseball park, where they pried the boards off the fence and used them to build a big pyre in the middle of the field. Right there they burned up what was left of Willie Reed.

Josh's train arrived Wednesday night in Miami. The next morning he boarded a Pan Am seaplane, which took him to the mouth of the Higuamo River in San Pedro de Macorís.

After losing Satchel and his fellow stars, Negro League fans had tightly embraced the good news that "the hands-across-the-Caribbean ha[d] not succeeded in snatching the league's most famous home run hitter, Josh Gibson of the Homestead Grays . . . the Babe Ruth of the Negro league."[1] With Josh now gone, Negro League fans had lost their last shred of consolation.

· · ·

It was a day near the end of May when panic spread through the ranks of the Dragones about an item that had appeared on the sports page claiming Josh Gibson was on a steamship headed for the Dominican Republic to play for the rival Águilas.[2] The Dragones' fears were well founded. Everyone knew that Josh and Dihigo were friends from the days when they had played together on the 1934 Venezuelan Concordia club. They had all witnessed Josh's inhuman power that year when the Concordia club played in the capital city against Licey and Escogido. And for years Latin America would talk about Josh's power displays at Escambron Stadium in San Juan, where it had become a custom to send stadium workers climbing up the trees ringing the stadium to mark the spots that Josh hit with glittering ornaments. After a few seasons some of the trees—

which stood in a ring fifty feet from the outfield fence, some nearly five hundred feet from home plate—were as decorated as Christmas trees.[3]

Aybar sprang into action. Early on Wednesday morning he roused Satchel at his club. They walked over to dentist's office, where they spent all day firing off telegrams and making telephone calls to discover the truth. To their immense relief they learned that the rumor about Gibson going to a rival team was false. When the two got to the bottom of the "Josh-has-been-signed-by-Dihigo" rumor, they breathed a sigh of relief. Not losing a minute, the two kicked into high gear to sign him for the Dragones.

Landing Josh turned out to be trickier than bagging Satchel. Yes, Gibson wanted lots of money. But he wasn't willing to leave the Pittsburgh Homestead Grays until he had received proper clearance from his team's owner. A week of nervous waiting ensued. Finally word came that Josh would take $2,200 for the remaining seven weeks of the series.[4]

On Friday, the day before a critical game against the Estrellas, *Listín Diario* announced in a headline: "THE FAMOUS NO. AMERICAN PLAYER GIBSON ARRIVED YESTERDAY FOR 'CITY TRUJILLO B.B.C.'"[5]

On game day a large banner ad was splashed across the front page of *Listín* heralding the debut of Gibson. Even more prominently it featured the most naked pitch yet for Trujillo's reelection:

CAMPEONATO NACIONAL DE BASEBALL

"REELECCIÓN PRESIDENTE TRUJILLO"

ÚNICO JUEGO DE LA SEMANA

CIUDAD TRUJILLO VS. ESTRELLAS DE ORIENTE (National Baseball Championship for the "Reelection of President Trujillo" only game of the week Trujillo City vs. Eastern Stars.)

Debut del sensacional receptor J. GIBSON, en los "DRAGONES
DE CIUDAD TRUJILLO", champion batting de la Liga de Color
Americana ... (Debut of the sensational catcher J. Gibson,
of the Ciudad Trujillo Dragons, batting champion
of the American Negro League ...)

LA REELECCIÓN DEL PRESIDENTE TRUJILLO ES EL MAS
VEHEMENTE ANHELO DEL PUEBLO DOMINICANO.
(The reelection of President Trujillo is the most
vehement wish of the Dominican people.)[6]

In sync with the winding down of the national baseball
series, Trujillo kicked his more traditional reelection campaign
into high gear. Rallies again proliferated. Propaganda was prop-
agated. Near the end of June, the front page read: "HACIA LA
REELECCIÓN—UNA NECESIDAD NACIONAL" (Toward reelection—a national necessity). A banner across the entire bottom of the page screamed, "CAMPEONATO NACIONAL DE BASE
BALL "REELECCIÓN PRESIDENTE TRUJILLO" (National Baseball Championship for the Reelection of President Trujillo.)[7]

When Josh Gibson arrived, he displaced Satchel's buddy Cy
Perkins as the starting catcher for the Dragones. Their 3:00 p.m.
Saturday game against the Estrellas went eleven innings but
ended in a 2–2 tie after it was called for darkness.[8]

The following weekend—now the third weekend in June—
with the power-hitting Josh on board, the Dragones swept
through their games like a juggernaut. They took the Saturday game from the Águilas 5–3. And on Sunday the Dragones
swept aside the Estrellas twice by scores of 6–3 and 9–2. Josh
homered in the first game. Satchel shut down the Estrellas in
the second, holding them to two runs on six hits.[9]

When Monday morning came, Satchel's record stood at 5-1,
Josh had hit his first home run, and the Dragones had moved
back into first place in the standings at 13-11-1.[10]

The quick-starting Estrellas now fell to the bottom of the

1. The Dominican dictator Rafael Trujillo in 1936. From Besault, *President Trujillo*.

2. The capital city of the Dominican Republic, Santo Domingo, after the hurricane of 1930. A famous soothsayer told Trujillo that he would be swept into power by a hurricane—but also swept out by one. From Besault, *President Trujillo*.

3. The rebuilt and renamed capital city of the Dominican Republic, Ciudad Trujillo (Trujillo City). In the foreground is the one-quarter-sized replica of the Washington Monument—dedicated to Rafael Trujillo. Author's collection.

BOXING, TENNIS, GOLF
AND BASEBALL
BY EXPERTS

YOU'LL FIND THE LATEST
IN SPORTS EVENTS
IN THIS SECTION

PART TWO   CHICAGO, ILL., SATURDAY, MAY 1, 1937   PAGE THIRTEEN

PAIGE JUMPS CRAWFORDS

Golf Record, Meet To Bohannon

PERKINS ALSO SAID TO HAVE SKIPPED LOOP

Both Believed With Semi-Pro Nines In Canada

SHOOTS A 19 OVER COURSE FOR TRIUMPH

Charlie Adams, Victor In Playoff For 2 Place With 28

BIG GUNS IN MEMPHIS RED SOX' ATTACK

HOMER CURRY
Manager of the Memphis Red Sox baseball team who has been drilling his boys for the coming season. He is known for his excellent hitting and fielding.

NATE ROGERS

You May Not Know Lincoln In 1937; New Suits 'Tops'

Track Stars Shine In Annual Drake Relays

By EVERETT WADSWORTH
(Staff Correspondent)
DES MOINES, Iowa, April 30.

KANSAS CITY

---

4. Headline of the *Chicago Defender*, one of the dominant African American newspapers in the 1930s. *Chicago Defender*, May 1, 1937.

5. The baseball stadium in Ciudad Trujillo, located on the shore of the Caribbean. Satchel Paige thought it "looked something like a bull ring." Archivo General de la Nación de República Dominicana, Santo Domingo.

6. The rusting hulk of the American cruiser USS *Memphis*, a relic of the 1916 American invasion, which sat stranded on the shore of the Caribbean just beyond the right-field fence of the baseball stadium. Author's collection.

7. Lina Lovatón, Trujillo's handpicked
queen of the 1937 carnival and
his soon-to-be mistress. Archivo
General de la Nación de República
Dominicana, Santo Domingo.

8. Martín "El Maestro" Dihigo arrives as savior of the Santiago Eagles. *La Tribuna*, July 13, 1937, in Archivo General de la Nación de República Dominicana, Santo Domingo.

9. Cartoon from a contemporary Dominican newspaper of Satchell Paige and Andrews chatting it up before a game. *La Tribuna*, May 21, 1937, in Archivo General de la Nación de República Dominicana, Santo Domingo.

10. A front-page ad for the game between the Dragones de Ciudad Trujillo and the Estrellas de Oriente announcing the debut of Josh Gibson and promoting "the reelection of President Trujillo, which is the most vehement wish of the Dominican people." *Listín Diario*, June 12, 1937.

11. Dr. José Enrique Aybar (center) with the Dragones de Ciudad Trujillo. Author's collection.

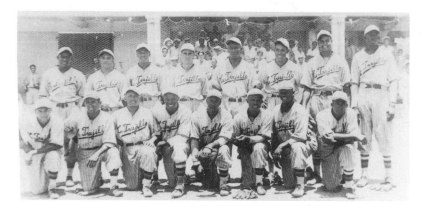

12. The Dragones at their stadium in Ciudad Trujillo. Satchel Paige is the tallest player on the far right. Author's collection.

13. Satchel Paige, Griffin, Fernández, and Leroy Matlock, the four major pitchers for the Dragones de Ciudad Trujillo. Author's collection.

14. Satchel Paige as depicted in a Dominican newspaper during the 1937 series. *La Tribuna*, May 3, 1937, in Archivo General de la Nación de República Dominicana, Santo Domingo.

15. Satchel Paige with his two catchers, Josh Gibson and Cy Perkins. Author's collection.

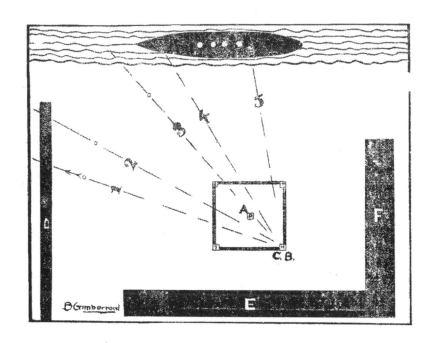

TRY COLORED PITCHERS

THE PRODIGAL SONS RETURN

"BETWEEN JOHN HENRY LEWIS AND BASEBALL, GUS STAYS IN THE MIDDLE"

GUS GREENLEE

GUS AND THE NEGRO-NATIONAL LEAGUE BIGWIGS HAVE FORGIVEN THE SAN DOMINGO CONTRACT JUMPERS. NOW WHERE WILL COLORED BASEBALL GO THIS YEAR, THE FANS WAIL.

16. (*opposite top*) The flight of the balls out of the stadium in Ciudad Trujillo onto Piña Street and the deck of the abandoned USS *Memphis* over the right-field fence. *La Tribuna*, June 30, 1937, in Archivo General de la Nación de República Dominicana, Santo Domingo.

17. (*opposite bottom*) A cartoon in the *Afro-American* after the World Series in October 1937 showing the Giants' star pitcher Carl Hubbell getting shelled by Joe DiMaggio with the less-than-subtle hint: "Try Colored Pitchers." *Afro-American*, October 16, 1937.

18. (*above*) Gus Greenlee forgiving the "San Domingo 'contract jumpers.'" Greenlee's forgiveness of Satchel Paige turned out to be short-lived, for his star pitcher soon afterward signed to pitch in the Mexican league. *Afro-American*, March 26, 1938.

19. Trujillo's one-quarter-sized replica of the Washington Monument as it stands today dedicated to and decorated with murals of the Mirabal sisters, who were murdered on Trujillo's orders in 1960. Author's collection.

20. Trujillo's light-blue 1957 Chevrolet Bel Air sitting riddled with bullets following his assassination in 1961. Archivo General de la Nación de República Dominicana, Santo Domingo.

standings. Their problems had been building since the failed recruiting trip to Pittsburgh, which netted jail time but no Negro Leaguers. To make matters worse, at the beginning of June, Estrellas star pitcher Ramón Bragaña was suspended for ten days over a spat with an umpire.[11] Then on the same day Josh Gibson arrived, three of their key players left on a steamship headed back to Cuba.[12]

A final humbling of the defending champion Estrellas came after the late-June weekend sweep by the Dragones. Just as the two capital teams had been forced out of the series the previous year, the Estrellas were summarily dropped from the tourney when it became mathematically impossible for them to win.[13] It put a smile on Trujillo's face when he read the nasty parting kick at the annoying upstarts from the East: "The team of San Pedro de Macorís (q.e.p.d). has beaten the record for having most names. They go by 'Stars of East,' 'Champions,' 'Eastern Elephants,' 'Pachyderms,' 'Protestant Stars,' 'Los de Siempre,' and now posthumously, 'Putrid Elephants.'"[14]

With the fall of the Estrellas, the schedule was reshuffled to book three games between the Dragones and the Águilas on the last weekend of June, three on the first weekend of July, and a game on Saturday, July 11, with additional games to be scheduled if necessary.

Now the two teams facing each other for the crown were radically different from the ones that had started the season. The Dragones had started the season with three Dominicans, five Cubans, one Puerto Rican, and no Americans. Their closing game lineup featured six American Negro Leaguers and three Cubans. Of the nine players only two of the Cubans had played in the opening game.

Likewise the Águilas had started the season with four Dominicans and five Cubans. Their closing game lineup included only three of the original nine players: Horacio Martínez at shortstop, Bragañita García at second, and Santos Amaro at first. The final lineup card had five Americans from the Negro Leagues, two Cubans, and two Dominicans.

The 1937 Águilas Cibaeñas
(in batting order from final game)

Clyde "Big Splo" Spearman, RF—From Arkadelphia (halfway between Little Rock and Texarkana), Arkansas. Bats left, throws right. A .300 hitter with power, above-average speed, and good defense.

Horacio "Rabbit" Martínez, SS—From Santo Domingo, Dominican Republic. Bats right, throws right. World-class defensive shortstop, an average hitter with good speed and bunting skills.

Santos "Kangaroo" Amaro, 3B—From Aguacate (in the middle of the island between Havana and Matzanas), Cuba. Bats right, throws right. Known as "El Kangaroo" for his extraordinary leaping ability. A .300 + hitter with power to the gaps. Member of the Mexican Baseball Hall of Fame.

Roy "Red" Parnell, LF—From Austin, Texas. Bats right, throws right. Solid defensive outfielder, .300 hitter with occasional power. He appeared twice in the East-West Negro League All Star games.

Martín "El Maestro" Dihigo, CF, P—From Matanzas, Cuba. Bats right, throws right. Broadly recognized as the best all-round player to ever play the game. He could hit for average plus power, was outstanding defensively, and possessed a strong arm and great speed. In his later years became a dominant pitcher. Only player to be a member of the American, the Cuban, the Mexican, the Dominican, the Venezuelan, and the Latin American Halls of Fame.

Robert "Spoony" Palm, c—From Clarendon (to the east of Little Rock on the way to Memphis), Arkansas. Bats right, throws right. Decent catcher with power. In his best seasons he hit over .300.

David "Showboat" Thomas, 1B—From Mobile, Alabama. Bats left, throws left. Ultra-smooth fielding first baseman with flash thrown in. He frequently took throws at first base behind his back; his signature play was to make a behind-the-back catch on an inning-ending 3-6-3 double play. In his best seasons in the Negro Leagues (1935–38), he hit in the .280 range with slight power.

Juan Delfino "Bragañita" García, 2B—From Moca, Dominican Republic. Fluid defensive infielder who could hit for average.

Chester Arthur "Chet" Brewer, p—From Leavenworth, Kansas. Bats switch, throws right. A control pitcher with a wide variety of pitches including a live fastball, big curve, screwball, emery ball, sinker, and overhand drop ball. His best season as a pro was in 1938 playing for the Mexican League; he posted an 18-3 record with a 1.82 ERA.

Other Notable Players

Andrew "Pat" Patterson, IF—From Chicago, Illinois. Bats switch, throws right. Utility infielder with good contact, speed, and occasional power.

Avelino "Belito" Alvarez, OF—From Cuba. A solid .290 hitter in the 1937 championship series.

Bertrum "Bert" or "Buffalo" Hunter, p—From Phoenix, Arizona. Bats right, throws right. Known as a master of the curve ball, he was a Negro League star of the 1930s. During the 1937 championship series, he met and married a Dominican woman.

Luis Eleuterio "Sir Skinny" or "Lefty" Tiant Sr., P—From Havana, Cuba. Bats left, throw left. A crafty lefthander with control, deceptive motion, change of speed, decent fastball, and devastating curve. He is in the Cuban Baseball Hall of Fame and was the father of Luis Tiant of Major League fame.

The 1937 Dragones de Ciudad Trujillo (in batting order from final game)

James "Cool Papa" Bell, CF—From Starkville (in the northeast near the Alabama border), Mississippi. Bats switch, throws left. Likely the fastest player to ever put on a baseball uniform. His maternal great grandfather was a full-blooded Native American from Oklahoma whose son married an African American woman.[15] His father's side was African American. At his peak he batted in a range from .320 to .350; at times he was in the .400 range, with a high mix of extra base hits mixed with occasional power. He was also a fine defensive outfielder. Member of the American Baseball Hall of Fame.

Harry Williams, 2B—From Pittsburgh, Pennsylvania. Bats right, throws right. A versatile infielder who could hit for average with some power.

Lázaro Salazar, 1B—From Havana, Cuba. Bats left, throws left. Like Dihigo an excellent hitter and pitcher. Salazar often posted winning seasons as a pitcher while posting above .300 hitting marks. Member of the Cuban and the Venezuelan Halls of Fame.

Joshua "Josh" Gibson, C—From Buena Vista, Georgia. Bats right, throws right. The "Black Babe Ruth." Without question the most powerful bat of his generation. Gibson also hit for high average, at times exceeding .400. A better-than-average catcher with a rifle arm. Member of the American Baseball Hall of Fame.

Samuel "Sammy" Bankhead, ss—From Sulligent (in the northwest corner near the Mississippi border), Alabama. Bats right, throws right. Outstanding defensive player with above-average speed plus the ability to hit for average. As a teenager he worked in the Alabama coal mines but played baseball on the side. In 1951 he became the first black coach in Minor League Baseball.

William "Cy" Perkins, RF, C—From Georgia. Bats right, throws right. Perkins was Satchel Paige's catcher of choice. He wore a chest protector painted with the Seventh Commandment: "Thou Shalt Not Steal." An excellent defensive catcher with a strong arm, he had seasons when he hit as high as .300 and always had decent power.

Antonio "Tony" Castaño, LF—From Palma Soriano (at the extreme eastern tip of the island near Guantanamo), Cuba. Bats right, throws right. A .280 to .300 hitter with solid defensive skills.

Marceline "Cho-Cho" Correa, 3B—From Cuba. Bats right, throws right. Above-average defensive infielder with a batting average that tended to hover around the .270 mark.

Leroy Matlock, P—From Moberly (halfway between Kansas City and St. Louis), Missouri. Bats left, throws left. Star left-handed pitcher with an above-average fastball, curve, drop, change-up, screwball, and slider. Over a thirteen-year career he almost always posted a winning season with a strong ERA.

Other Notable Players

Leroy "Satchel" Paige, P—From Mobile, Alabama. Bats right, throws right. Legendary pitcher now in the American Baseball Hall of Fame.

Perucho "The Bull" Cepeda, 1B, SS—From San Juan, Puerto Rico. Bats right, throws right. A star infielder, he could hit with significant power while maintaining a high batting average—he had seasons over .350. He refused to play in the United State because of the endemic racism. He is a member of the Puerto Rican Baseball Hall of Fame and was the father of Orlando Cepeda of Major League fame.

Silvio García, IF, P—From Limonar (just to the east of Matanzas), Cuba. Bats right, throws right. An all-round player who could fill in at any position. An excellent hitter he posted averages above .350 and provided speed on the bases.

Robert "Schoolboy" Griffith, P—From Liberty (to the east of Nashville), Tennessee. Throws right, bats right. A six-feet-five power pitcher with a nasty spitball, he could also hit for power when given a chance.

15

Fiesta de la Chapita

They opened the front door of their club and wandered out into the morning heat wearing swimsuits with towels lazily slung over their shoulders, all nine of them   Satchel, Cy, Jabbo, Schoolboy, Cool Papa, Harry, Leroy, Josh, and Sammy. Josh and Sammy joined in, but hung behind the others, chewing on a conversation of their own.

After a few blocks the nine men ran into the wide street by the ocean lined with the big palm trees. They turned left to walk toward the mouth of the river, where the pier was. When Cool Papa turned his back, Satchel pushed him into the water. A happy ruckus ensued with each one throwing the other into the warm ocean. Once they were all in the water, they splashed the morning away. Of course the soldier with the gun stoically watched them, but they didn't much mind the daytime guy. He was friendly, much better than the nasty one, with the non-stop scowl, who came at night.

When they returned to the club, lunch had been laid out for them on a long table: chicken soup, potatoes, beans, rice, fried plantains, and pineapple with coffee to finish. At 2:00 p.m. the nine were chaperoned to practice at the ballpark for the afternoon. Since the little doctor had taken over, these practices had become serious, even strenuous, ordeals. It turned out that he had watched the thorough practices of an American Minor League team from Richmond, Virginia, in 1933. He marveled at and then copied the way this team had systematically broken out the various aspects of batting and fielding into drills and workouts.[1]

But all in all, compared to the constant travel of the Negro Leagues, even this regimen was a breeze. After practice in the late afternoon, the nine enjoyed food and people-watching at Café Hollywood on Calle El Conde. Now that they were always followed by Señor Paulino's guards, they played endless games of cards into the night.

Sammy and Josh were the only two who figured out how to occasionally sneak away at night for beers. Their advantage over Satchel's posse of seven was their naturally low-key personalities and discretion in keeping everyone else—Satchel most of all—in the dark.[2]

Going into the weekend's games, Josh was singled out for praise. "Since the great Gibson donned the uniform of the Ciudad Trujillo Dragones," a *Listín Diario* columnist wrote, "things have changed like night and day." Josh's impact was compared to Jesus raising Lazarus from the dead.[3] He wasn't far off; Josh's bat was the missing ingredient that had brought the Dragones to life.

It was now the end of June, and the two teams were headed into the first weekend of their two-team playoff for the championship. The Dragones stood at 13-11-1, the Águilas at 11-10.

On a hot Saturday afternoon the teams met to kick off the first weekend's playoff games. Aybar sat smiling from the first inning of the opening game, which quickly turned into a seventeen-hit, ten-run "massacre" of the Águilas, prompting *Listín Diario* to call the Dragones the "assassins of Calle El Conde." Josh had three hits, including a triple, and scored two runs. Cool Papa contributed two hits and scored three runs with his speed. Dragones lefthander Leroy Matlock took a five-hit shutout into the ninth, when Dihigo saved "their honor with home run," the only run of the day for the Águilas.[4]

Next morning at 9:00 a.m., after the 10–1 loss, Dihigo's team had the unenviable job of facing Satchel. To counter Satchel player/manager Dihigo called his own number to pitch. In the first inning the Águilas scratched out a run against Satchel, but that was all they would get. Satchel struck out eleven and hung an o for 3 on batter Dihigo. Dihigo stayed even with Satchel until the fourth inning, when he yielded a run in four consecutive frames to lose 5–1.[5]

Sunday's afternoon game was even worse. Schoolboy Griffith, a six-feet-five power pitcher with a nasty spitball from Liberty, Tennessee, held the Águilas to one hit to beat them 6–1. All the Dragones got into the action, pounding out twelve hits, tagging Luis "Sir Skinny" Tiant for six runs.[6]

After the first weekend the Dragones stood at 16-11-1, the Águilas 11-13. Paige led all pitchers with a mark of 6-1; Dihigo stood at 6-4.

• • •

Aybar kept reading and rereading the piece he had ordered up in *Listín Diario*—on himself. He especially loved the line, "That man, small in stature but with the heart and energy of a giant, was Dr. Joseph R. [*sic*] Aybar." But he also liked, "Last year . . . [when] Licey was shamefully defeated . . . Dr. Aybar had been ignored on this occasion" with its finger wagging "I-told-you-so" sentiment. After all why had everyone forgotten he was *the man* who had pulled off the impossible 1929 series win—after everyone had given up—with a seven-game winning streak. He reread the ending of the story several times. How true the statement that Dr. Aybar "imprints with his inexhaustible dynamism, with his iron discipline, with his notable intelligence, an amazing spirit among the Dragones and has put them, in less than a month, at the head of the National Championship."[7]

Suddenly the little dentist stopped and gulped. He had gotten so carried away reading praise of himself that he had forgotten to make sure the story had even more praise for Trujillo.

Okay, here it was: "benefactor," "golden age," "illustrious name," and so on. He counted the paragraphs and words, reassuring himself that the praise was sufficiently excessive.

Starting on Monday Aybar was eagerly anticipating the coming weekend series against the Águilas, when he just knew they would wrap up the championship. And as the week wore on, news of the Águilas' mounting troubles made him downright giddy. Midweek a rumor ran in *Listín Diario* that four of their Cuban players were heading home on a steamship—among them the brilliant Santos Amaro but also Belito Álvarez, Luis Tiant, and Cando López.[8]

Aybar arrived at the Campo Deportivo early to watch the teams practice before the game. Among the first players he saw when he sat down was Santos Amaro. He was spitting mad about the false rumor of Amaro leaving because aside from Dihigo, Santos was the most talented Cuban on the Águilas.

Debuting as Miss Sports 1937–38, Lourdes García Trujillo, Trujillo's niece, had the honor of throwing out the first ball for Saturday's game. Quick as lightening the Dragones struck with three runs in the bottom of the first. The Águilas closed the gap, scoring two in the top of the second. Going into the seventh the Dragones held a 6–5 lead, so the manager brought in Satchel to close out the game. He put up quick zeros in the seventh and eight as the Dragones built an 8–5 lead. The ninth was rough. Satchel barely survived after yielding two runs, but he held on for an 8–7 victory.[9]

For the little dentist this marked the eighth consecutive victory over the Águilas. Even better his recent acquisition, Josh Gibson, once again shone when he hit two more triples. Still he found it tremendously annoying that his spies had erroneously reported that Santos Amaro was leaving for Cuba. Santos had a four-hit day, which nearly beat the Dragones.

Bats, balls, equipment, players, victory speech, bus—the sun was going down when Aybar had finally acquitted his duties and hopped on the bus with his team. They made the now-familiar long drive over the mountains that night and arrived at their Santiago hotel to rest up for Sunday morning's game.

Sunday, July 4, 1937. The Dragones need one more win to clinch the championship. On this day at Play Enriquillo in Santiago, they had two chances. Schoolboy Griffith, who the previous weekend had one-hit the Águilas, was scheduled to start the morning game. Either it wasn't Schoolboy's day or Dihigo's team had figured him out; whatever the reason the Águilas exploded for six runs against the giant speed pitcher with the nasty spitter. Josh completed the cycle with a three-run homer in the ninth to draw the Dragones close, but they still they fell a run short, losing 8–7. Santos Amaro hit a home run, which was made the difference for the Águilas.[10]

Nonetheless, there was little question in Dr. Aybar's mind, with Satchel getting the start in the afternoon game, that they would clinch the series. Since his *pobre* series start, Satchel had been on a roll, winning eight times against just one loss and striking out eleven in his last start against the Águilas. The game quickly turned into a tough pitchers' duel between Satchel and Chet Brewer with Satchel losing for only the second time in the series by a 4–2 score.[11] Aybar tried his hardest not to show any concern over the two loses to the Águilas in Santiago.

Still, on his way back to Ciudad Trujillo, he spent every moment obsessively reassuring himself that everything would turn out right. After all they just needed to win one more game. Santiago needed to win two consecutive games. But every time he settled into a state of calmness, he was haunted by his own seven-game winning streak in the 1929 series—because he knew better than anyone, that it was possible. More than anything, the thought of heading into a sudden-death game with the Águilas, which was just a flip of the coin, simply made him sick.

The nine Negro Leaguers had never seen the *fanáticos* so excited, the fancy people so tight. Everywhere they walked during that week, people stopped and pointed. None of the nine understood much Spanish beyond what they needed to ask directions or order in a restaurant, yet in every conversation in the capital city that they overheard they picked out words like "baseball," "Dragones," "Satchel," "Águilas," "Josh," and "Dihigo."

Every day the newspapers were filled with gossip, stats, and profiles of the star players. Satchel and Josh had fun when the man who ran their favorite restaurant translated their newspaper profiles on the fly. Josh and his teammates got plenty of ribbing material when they discovered that the profile had called Satchel "Quixotic" and him "Babe Ruth."[12]

Fanáticos studied the stats. It was clear to them that Josh and Cool Papa were difference makers; in just twelve games Josh was hitting .420 with twenty-one hits, including four doubles, five triples, two home runs with twenty-one RBIS. Cool Papa was batting .323, but even more importantly he was using his great speed to score runs: thirteen runs in fifteen games.[13]

Meanwhile, Aybar kept hearing the elites grumble in hushed tones about the amount of money he had spent on the Dragones. It got to the point where he felt compelled to enlist the country's most respected sportswriter, Miguel A. Nadal (who wrote under the pseudonym HOMERUN), to silence this talk. "In baseball," HOMERUN wrote, "we believe in nothing more than three things: steadfastness, dynamism, and money. Fortunately, 'Ciudad Trujillo' has assembled the three. Hence we are in first place."[14]

A huge banner ran across the entire bottom of the newspaper in which the article appeared: "CAMPEONATO NACIONAL DE BASE BALL 'REELECCIÓN PRESIDENTE TRUJILLO,'" with the kicker "LOS DRAGONES PROCLAMAN LA REELECCIÓN DEL

PRESIDENTE TRUJILLO" (The Dragons support the reelection of President Trujillo).[15]

The soldiers enforcing the *mas estricto control* of Aybar's *nuevos rumbos* got tighter and tighter, meaner and meaner as the week wore on. Their boss, the man with the raven-black hair—Captain Paulino, they called him—set his men on edge by checking in with them constantly.

Late on Saturday night Águilas Negro League jumper Chet Brewer wandered down Calle El Conde. There he ran into a skinny young boy who he remembered ran errands for the Dragones. He asked the boy where the nine were. The boy looked up, with a don't-you-know smile and replied with a laugh, "They are in the *cárcel* [jail]."[16]

• • •

It was a splendid, hot, Sunday afternoon. Thousands of *fanáticos* streamed toward the Campo Deportivo from all points of the republic in buses, cars, and taxis. By Sunday morning the streets of Ciudad Trujillo were clogged with noisy partisans of the rival teams.

Satchel was partly miffed, partly relieved when he learned that fellow Negro Leaguer Leroy Matlock had been picked to start the Sunday game. It was true that last Saturday Matlock had pitched a sharp game, yielding just one run on a meaningless Dihigo home run in the ninth. But he was no Satchel Paige.

After batting practice and fielding drills, the manager called the Dragones together in the corner of their tiny dugout. Through his tight, severely serious mouth, he simply growled, "You better win."[17] As he walked the length of the dugout, Satchel hoped that today he would only be needed to root for his teammates.

All the *fanáticos* stood, roared, and waved their hats as the pinstriped Dragones took the field while Matlock tossed his warmup pitches to Josh.

From the start Chet Brewer and Leroy Matlock were locked in a scoreless duel and headed this way going into the bottom of the fifth inning. Out of the gate the Águilas grab the psychological edge with Brewer holding the Dragones hitless.

Dragones third baseman Cuco Correa started off the fifth by working Brewer for a walk. Then Matlock dropped down a sacrifice to move Cuco over. Brewer fielded the ball. He spun to throw to second trying to cut down the lead runner, but his throw sailed high, leaving both runners safe.

After two unsuccessful attempts, Cool Papa dropped down a sacrifice. Águilas shortstop Horacio, under extraordinary pressure from Cool Papa's speed, muffed the ball. The bases were now loaded as slumping second baseman Harry Williams walked to the plate. He stroked a single to center, scoring Cuco and Matlock. *Dragones 2, Águilas 0.* Cool Papa streaked to third on the play.

With Cool Papa at third and Williams at first, first baseman Lázaro Salazar ripped a single to center, scoring Cool Papa. *Dragones 3, Águilas 0.*

The crowd roared as the powerful Josh strode to the plate. He promptly scalded a ball to deep short for an infield hit, again loading the bases.

Dihigo coolly walked in from centerfield to take the ball from Brewer. He told the umpire he would be pitching. To calm the game down, Dihigo threw his warmup pitches like he had all the time in the world. He pushed the limits until he was reprimanded.

With the *fanáticos* somewhat quieted down by Dihigo's delay, Josh's friend shortstop Sammy Bankhead stepped up to the plate. A loud crack of the bat resounded through the stadium. Deafening screams of "Hurrah" followed the flight of the ball out of the stadium onto Calle Pina, where it bounced on the pavement. Four runners crossed home plate—or what the newspaper would call "el pentágono de las angustias," "the pentagon of anguish."[18] *Dragones 7, Águilas 0.*

The inning seemed to be winding down as Cy and Castaño hit into easy outs. When Cuco came to bat for a second time, he beat out an infield hit. Thanks to the second baseman's error, he took second on the play. Leroy Matlock hit a double, scoring Cuco. *Dragones 8, Águilas 0.*

Satchel watched with growing relief as Leroy Matlock cut through the Águilas lineup using his great control to mix sharp fastballs with curves, drops, screwballs, and sliders. Almost before he knew it, they were coasting into the ninth with an 8–2 lead.

It's hard to tell if Matlock had run out of gas, if the hitters had figured him out, or if the sight of armed soldiers lined up in plain view was unnerving him, but suddenly he was hittable. In the twinkling of an eye, the championship game was in a state of collapse.

Single—double—single. Slick fielding first baseman David "Showboat" Thomas began the rally with a single for the Águilas. Then García doubled. Next Big Splo Spearman walked to the plate. There was one out. Águilas were standing on first and third. Big Splo singled to drive in a run. *Dragones 8, Águilas 3.*

The manager stood, growled, craned his neck to look down the length of the dugout where Satchel was trying to keep out of sight. "Ven acá," he spat. In utter dread Satchel hastily warmed up. He was summoned to pitch. As he walked to the mound, all he could think of were those soldiers standing in foul territory with long knives and guns in their belts; he knew that "they could use them." Standing on the mound he felt so jittery that even as he talked to himself he was stuttering: "L-l-l-listen S-s-s-atch, pull yourself together before they air-condition you." It was small comfort to the tall, lanky right-hander that anything he threw near the plate would be called a strike "'cause the umpires saw the guns too."[19]

Satchel's shattered nerves took a toll on his confidence. He quickly thought things through as clearly as he could. The first two hitters he would face were Pat Patterson and Santos Amaro. He had played with Patterson on the Pittsburgh Crawfords, so he knew that the speedy switch hitter could beat out almost any grounder to the hole. Next up would be the tall, powerful, right-handed-hitting Cuban Santos Amaro. "El Canguro" was a different matter altogether. Satchel feared his power; he had already homered four times in this series.

Patterson touched Satchel for a single. *Dragones 8, Águilas 4*.

El Canguro walked to the plate taking warmup cuts. He stroked another single. *Dragones 8, Águilas 5*.

Satchel finally got a break. He induced Philadelphia Star jumper Roy "Red" Parnell to ground into a force at second.

Two outs.

Cuban slugger Martín Dihigo strode to the plate next waving a bat in his hands. The sportswriter for *Listín Diario* later recounted what every *fanático* in the stadium was thinking: if Dihigo, who led the league in homers and had hit three off Satchel got ahold of one, the game would be tied. With first base open, Satchel could walk Dihigo if he chose. Yet he decided to pitch to him.

Dihigo singled, driving in Pat Patterson. *Dragones 8, Águilas 6*.

Parnell now stood at third. Dihigo took a healthy lead at first with his team down only two runs.

Standing on the mound Satchel looked down at his feet. He closed his eyes for a split second to take stock. He felt sick to his stomach knowing that the outcome of this game was bigger than baseball.

Águilas catcher Spoony Palm, who had three doubles and a home run in the series, walked to the plate representing the go-ahead run. Satchel fired. Spoony slashed a sharp grounder to deep short. Shortstop Sammy Bankhead made a sensational play to glove the ball but sent an offline throw to first. Dragones first baseman Salazar lunged to make a tough catch to end the game.

• • •

In a flash the little dentist came running onto the field. He led the team in an impromptu triumphal procession around the Campo Deportivo to the cheers of the jubilant crowd. Together they were swept out of the stadium by the multitude up to Parque Independencia, then down Calle El Conde. A parade of sorts formed as they ambled and waved their caps.

A vast, boisterous crowd amassed in front of the Ciudad Trujillo Baseball Club offices on Calle El Conde to celebrate the victory. The crowd swayed to the beats of the touring band Marcano, which had set up just outside the door.

Meanwhile, another victory party got under way at the home of sportswriter Miguel Nadal for the Dragones directors, sports sportswriters, VIP team boosters, and civic leaders. "Repeated toasts of foaming beer" interrupted the loud affair.[20]

A letter was read by a representative of the Santiago Águilas:

HON. PRESIDENT TRUJILLO,

PRESIDENTIAL MANSION:

We have the high honor of informing you of the completion of the Baseball Championship for the Reelection of President Trujillo, with a resounding victory for the sports colors of this city, which is dignified by your distinguished name. Both Santiago and Ciudad Trujillo join in this moment with common cordiality, such aspiration it is that of anticipating the glorious victory of the reelection of the most important president who has served this republic for the good of the homeland for the present and for the future, we express to you the feelings of deepest admiration and friendship.[21]

Dr. Aybar took out his folded speech, which had been sitting in his pocket for nearly two weeks, and read it aloud: "We have gone to the Honorable President Trujillo and informed him of the victory of 'Ciudad Trujillo,' and we embraced each other in the greatest cordiality. Simultaneously we told the distinguished chief the necessity of his reelection, for the good of the homeland, for the present and for the future. We all embrace him."[22]

They brought forward Trujillo's eight-year-old son, Ramfis, or, to be exact, Colonel Rafael L. Trujillo Martínez. To wild cheers Aybar presented the colonel with the championship trophy, in appropriately florid language: "Colonel, champions already, I offer you this trophy as the highest award of the city that is honored by the august name of your distinguished father. Our city embraces you."[23]

All at once the nine noticed that Paulino's men had melted away. *Mas estricto control* was over and done. *Nuevos rumbos* was now yesterday's news. Satchel, Cy, Schoolboy, Cool Papa, Harry, Leroy, Josh, and Sammy cut loose. It was open season on bars, hotels, fiestas, and *casas de chicas*. Not only was no one afraid any longer to sell them a drink; hell, they were plying them with free hard stuff quicker than they could drink it.

When the nine attained a semblance of sobriety, they were treated to a picnic at one of Trujillo's plantations.[24] Bert "Buffalo" Hunter, one of the Negro League jumpers for the Águilas, found love in the Dominican Republic during the Campeonato. He married a Dominican woman and stayed on the island, using it as a base to play in the Mexican leagues during the early 1940s.[25]

The very next day the little dentist held a closing press conference aimed at the American press. Aybar, whom Satchel described as "one of those fellows who never stops once he starts talking," opined, "It is the general opinion here that all the imported players in this city are the best in the world. It is my personal opinion that if our team which won the championship met any white league team, our team would win." [26]

Then Aybar fibbed: "Money makes no difference. Baseball is spiritual in every aspect, as indulged in by the Latin races." The little dentist finished with an oblique shot at American racism: "This is the most hospitable town in Latin America. All courtesies will be shown visitors—especially colored Americans."[27]

• • •

The men arrived at the presidential palace on the Wednesday before the championship game. They were told to wait. Waiting meant standing, sweating, and worrying outside Trujillo's office. Nearly half an hour had gone by when the door suddenly opened. Trujillo motioned for them to come in for a short talk about the upcoming reelection campaign.

Everyone in the room knew they hadn't yet won the championship. What Trujillo really must have meant was "when they did, as expected, win the championship."

The rest of the meeting was devoted to the details of the reelection campaign—things like publishing a manifesto, planning mass rallies, organizing the provinces, ensuring the blessing of the churches.

Aybar was charged with publishing the manifesto. Like clockwork the headline of *Listín Diario* on the Tuesday after the championship game blared:

MANIFESTO PRO REELECCIÓN DEL PDTE. TRUJILLO Q. LANZA JUVENTUD UNIVERSITARIA.[28]

[Manifesto for the reelection of President Trujillo led by university youth]

Table 1. Box score for championship game Campo Deportivo Municipal, Ciudad Trujillo, Sunday, July 11, 1937

Sumario del Juego Final del Campeonato de Base Ball Nacional Celebrado El Domingo 11

Águilas Cibaeñas	AB	R.	H.	O.	A.	E.
Spearman, RF	5	1	2	2	0	0
Horacio, SS	4	1	1	4	2	1
x Patterson.	1	1	1	0	0	0
Amaro, 3B	5	1	2	1	2	0
Parnell, LF	5	0	1	2	0	0
Dihigo, CF, P	5	0	4	0	2	0
Palm, C	4	0	0	1	1	0
Thomas, 1B	4	1	3	13	1	0
B. García, 2B	3	1	2	1	6	1
Brewer, P	2	0	0	0	0	1
xx Alvarez, CF	1	0	0	0	0	1
	39	6	16	24	14	4

x Bateo por Horacio en el 9º. xx Jugo per Brewer desde el 5º.

Ciudad Trujillo	AB	R.	H.	O.	A.	E.
Bell, CF	4	1	1	3	1	1
William, 2B	5	1	1	3	3	0
Salazar, 1B	4	1	1	11	1	0
Gibson, C	4	1	3	4	1	0
Bankhead, SS	5	1	1	3	6	1
Perkins, RF	4	0	1	1	0	0
Castaño, LF	4	0	1	1	0	0
x Vargas, LF	0	0	0	0	0	0
Correa, 3B	2	2	1	0	0	0
Matlock, P	3	1	1	1	3	0
xx Paige, P	0	0	0	0	0	0
	33	8	11	27	15	2

x Jugo por Castaño en el 8º. xx Pitcheo por Matlock en el 9º.

• • •

Águilas Cibaeñas	000	002	004
Ciudad Trujillo	000	080	00x

• • •

Home Run: Sammy Bankhead

Doubles: Amaro, Dihigo, Matlock

Runs Batted In: Bankhead 4, Amaro 2, Williams 2, Salazar 1, Matlock 1, Palm 1, B. García 1, Patterson 1, Dihigo 1

Sacrifice Hits: Matlock, B. García

Innings Pitched: por Brewer 4, por Dihigo 4, por Matlock 8 y tercio. Por Paige dos tercios.

Strike Outs: Dihigo 1, por Matlock 4

Bases on Balls: Brewer 2, Dihigo 2, Matlock 2

Passed Ball: Palm 1

Wild Pitch: Brewer 1

Time: 2 horas 35 minutos

Chief Umpire: Eustaquio Gutierrez. Bases: Libio Guerra

Official Scorekeeper: Manuel A. Salazar.

Table 2. Average Batting de los jugadores que tomaron parte en Campeonato "Reelección Presidente Trujillo" (Batting averages of the players who took part in the Championship for the "Reelection of President Trujillo")

RECORD OFICIAL

Player	T	G	AB	R	H	2B	3B	HR	RBI	SO	ERROR	AVG
Joshua Gibson	CT	13	53	10	24	4	5	2	21	8	12	.453
Clyde Spearman	AC	19	71	15	25	4	0	0	7	5	2	.352
Martín Dihigo	AC	25	97	18	34	6	2	4	19	16	4	.351
Pat Patterson	AC	13	47	7	15	1	0	0	3	7	7	.319
Cool Papa Bell	CT	16	66	14	21	4	3	0	3	10	1	.318
Ramón Bragaña	EO	21	74	12	23	3	0	3	11	18	6	.311
Santos Amaro	AC	27	110	19	34	3	3	4	19	12	8	.309
Sammy Bankhead	CT	17	68	10	21	1	0	2	13	9	9	.309
Silvio García	CT	31	128	26	38	14	1	0	20	11	23	.297
George Scales	EO	11	44	7	13	2	0	0	1	4	4	.295
Lázaro Salazar	CT	30	120	31	35	2	5	0	17	8	6	.292
Belito Alvarez	AC	27	94	19	27	6	0	0	9	4	2	.287
Roy Parnell	AC	12	46	4	13	1	0	1	7	6	2	.283
Tetelo Vargas	EO	26	106	22	30	6	2	0	5	9	5	.283
Cando López	AC	19	60	7	17	4	0	0	4	6	0	.283
Tony Castaños	CT	14	45	7	12	2	1	0	3	4	3	.267

Name												
Enrique Lantigua	CT	20	57	7	15	3	0	0	2	5	10	.263
Radamés López	EO	25	96	11	25	6	0	1	10	12	6	.260
Herman Andrews	CT	12	43	1	11	4	0	0	4	20	2	.255
Clarence Palm	AC	20	71	12	18	3	0	1	11	11	7	.254
Cocaína García	EO	25	63	4	16	3	0	0	5	3	4	.254
Cy Perkins	CT	26	99	7	25	5	0	0	13	9	9	.253
Pedro Arango	EO	36	99	7	24	2	1	1	8	12	7	.250
Alejandro Oms	EO	26	99	10	23	4	2	0	9	7	3	.232
Horacio Martínez	AC	28	114	14	26	5	1	1	15	11	22	.228
Harry Williams	CT	16	66	9	15	1	0	0	12	4	9	.227
Mellizo Puesán	EO	20	40	5	9	3	0	0	10	5	2	.225
Julio Rojo	EO	25	92	6	20	1	3	0	5	10	6	.217
Carlos Blanco	EO	21	74	8	16	3	0	0	10	9	5	.216
Sonlly Alvarado	CT	17	46	3	9	1	0	0	3	9	7	.196
Mon Ruiz	EO	13	40	3	7	0	1	0	4	11	3	.175
Huesito Vargas	CT	23	80	11	13	3	1	1	5	12	4	.163
David Thomas	AC	19	76	6	12	3	0	0	9	16	6	.158
Bragañita García	AC	20	55	2	8	0	0	0	3	4	5	.145
Miguel Solis	CT	16	47	4	5	1	0	0	3	6	7	.105

Adapted from *Listín Diario*, July 19, 1937, and Cordova, *El campeonato de 1937*, 57. Because the statistics were originally computed with paper and pencil, some did not add up accurately.

16

The Maestro's Coda

Dihigo could still hear the cheering and shouting following the championship game as he changed into his street clothes after the game. When he left the stadium, he walked east along El Malecón to avoid the crowd, which was heading north. He returned unimpeded to his hotel in the colonial district of Ciudad Trujillo.

Shortly afterward Dihigo bought a ticket on a steamer headed for Havana that was departing from Trujillo's sparkling new port. The always-cheerful Dihigo was especially pleased to be greeted at the Havana port by his beautiful wife, Africa. In the following weeks he talked the business of baseball. After long negotiations at cafés in Havana, he decided to play for the Marianao club that winter in Cuba. He realized he could still shoehorn in an intriguing offer from the fledgling Mexican league. The Águila of Veracruz had offered him a handsome salary to help the club finish out its season.

On a sunny tropical morning, he kissed his wife good-bye and headed back to the dock to catch a steamer headed for Veracruz. Soon, standing on the top deck, he caught sight of the Mexican coastline, shadowed by sharply rising mountains above the coastal plane. As the boat entered the harbor, Dihigo's attention was grabbed by dozens of a huge black birds circling overhead. He looked closer and was astonished to discover that they were buzzards. Even more buzzards were flopping around in the shallow water, dolefully flapping their long black wings and crying out as Dihigo's steamer docked. Dihigo walked down the gangplank where porters swarmed him, practically seizing his bags. He quickly discovered that he was expected to relinquish his bags and was legally required to pay a charge of one peso per piece of luggage.

At the pier Dihigo hailed a taxi to take him to the Hotel Diligencia. It didn't take him long to unpack his bags and begin wandering the streets of this new city. His first trip was to the arcade packed with food stands and souvenir stores that ran below the Rexes Hotel. As he walked, he was shocked by how hot this town was despite being on the ocean. Again he noticed black buzzards, perched on housetops and waddling around the streets. Later that night he wandered through the city. It surprised him how many black people he saw. And to his surprise, he found that many of them were Cubans. Everywhere he walked, he heard Cuban music, in the parks, in the streets, spilling out of open windows. Dihigo returned to the arcade to buy a piece of red snapper that had been fried in brown paper. He peeled off the paper, which took the skin off with it, spread some butter over the white meat, dusted it with a little pepper, and enjoyed himself thoroughly. It began to rain while Dihigo was walking back to his hotel. That night he fell asleep reading a book under his mosquito net.

That next morning Dihigo had breakfast with his new manager, fellow Cuban Agustin Verde, who gave him the rundown on the team. The Águila was composed of talented but unheralded young Mexican players who played with great athletic ability. What they needed was help in sharpening their baseball skills. Verde asked Dihigo both to teach his young players and to pitch as many of the seven games left in the season as he could manage.

No one in the Mexican League had ever seen an arm like Dihigo's. Right away he gunned down the first runner to test his arm from center field. "Out," yelled the umpire. Dihigo fell down laughing with the remark, "You no run on me, boy, you no run on me."[1] Runners who were used to taking extra bases quickly learned better.

When Dihigo took the mound for the Águila, he simply overwhelmed the Mexican hitters. His pitches so utterly baffled opposing batters' fans that they took to calling them *jeroglíficos* (hieroglyphs). On September 16, 1937, he pitched the first no-hitter in Mexican League history. It was a 4–0 gem over Nogales in Veracruz. And for the first time the Águila won the Mexican League championship. Dihigo played in seven games—in twenty-eight at bats, he hit .357 with one double, two triples, and one home run. As a pitcher he went 4-0 with a 0.93 ERA. In 38⅔ innings, he struck out fifty-eight batters against just eight walks.

The following year Dihigo returned to Mexico to again play for his friend Agustin Verde's Veracruz team. The team from Mexico City, Agrario, cooked up its own plan to counter Dihigo and wrest the Mexican League championship away from Veracruz. The team signed Satchel Paige. The first duel between Dihigo and Paige took place on September 5, 1938. With his blazing fastballs mixed in with his nasty curveballs, Dihigo shut down the Agrario. Satchel left with the game tied 1–1 in the seventh. Dihigo stepped to the plate in the top of the ninth and dramatically clubbed the reliever's offering over the left-field fence and into a distant meadow for a 3–1 lead.[2] He stuck out the three final batters to end the game.

Satchel and Dihigo dueled for the last time in Mexico City on September 18, 1938. On that day Satchel pitched with a damaged arm and was crushed 10–3 by Dihigo's team.[3] Dihigo, went 6 for 6 with a home run, an extra base hit, and four singles— marking the first time that a 6 for 6 had been posted in the league. When the season ended, the Veracruz Águila was again champion, and Dihigo had won eighteen games against two losses, posted a 0.90 ERA, struck out 184 in 167 innings, and hit .387. This was the second time in his career (the 1935–36 Cuban season was the other) in which he won both the batting crown and all pitching titles (strikeouts, wins, and ERA).

Dihigo did not retire until 1947 at age forty-one. Once he returned to Cuba, he worked as a sports journalist for a socialist paper. When Colonel Fulgencio Batista seized power in a coup d'état in 1952, Dihigo left Cuba for Mexico as a personal protest against the new military dictatorship. He vowed that he would not return to Cuba until the tyrant fell.[4]

Back in Mexico Dihigo only agreed to put his baseball uniform back on to play in an exhibition game to raise money for Castro's Cuban revolution. Thus when Fidel Castro shocked the world by overthrowing the dictator Batista on January 1, 1959, Dihigo sailed back to Cuba to settle in Havana. At once Castro named him minister of sports and put him in charge of reorganizing baseball and physical-education programs.[5]

Dihigo died on his sixty-fifth birthday in Cienfuegos, Cuba. One Cuban newspaper eulogized him: "A big old heart has stopped beating. Baseball, in a moment, lost one of its most extraordinary figures, and although Cooperstown has not properly recognized him, every great player has his rightful place in his homeland. We, both old and young, will place his coffin in our own land, with many lips exclaiming, 'Gracias, Inmortal!'"[6] The *Miami Herald* simply wrote, "Martin Dihigo, the man known as the greatest Cuban baseball player of all time, is dead."[7] As another Cuban newspaper sadly noted, "Dihigo was one of the many victims of racial discrimination in sports, which prevented him from showing his greatness in the so-called Major Leagues of baseball in the United States."[8]

It took another six years for Martín Dihigo to be inducted into America's Baseball Hall of Fame. In his lifetime he was known as either "El Inmortal" or "El Maestro." Fittingly he is the only player recognized by the American, Cuban, Mexican, Dominican, Venezuelan, and Latin American Baseball Halls of Fame.

17

The Heartbreaking End of Josh Gibson

Following the Dragones' victory, Josh and Sammy were swept out of the stadium and down Calle El Conde by the mob. Stuck in the bustle they were alternatively cheered, pushed, touched, kissed, hugged, and toasted. They stalled when the mob congealed in front of the Dragones headquarters to hear speeches from Dr. Aybar and a dignitary from Santiago. Finally they were swept into a bar with the other players. In the pandemonium they drank, chatted, and cheered toasts that they could only vaguely understand.

Once evening settled over Ciudad Trujillo, Josh and Sammy must have stolen away from the revelers and wandered down Calle Duarte to take refuge at Café Lindbergh so that they could be away from the nonstop chatter of Satchel and his cronies. For some time they probably sat in silence downing cerveza after cerveza. Since Sammy and Josh were such close friends, Sammy no doubt lobbied Josh to join him on Satchel's barnstorming tour.

As much as Josh would have loved to spend the rest of his summer hanging out with Sammy, he just couldn't square it with his promise to Cum Posey that he would return to Pittsburgh. They sadly parted ways that weekend after they attended a picnic at Trujillo's ranch. Josh took a Pan Am seaplane back to Miami, where he hopped on the train to Pittsburgh.

On Sunday, July 25, 1937, Josh arrived at Oriole Park in Baltimore for a doubleheader against the Washington Elites. Four thousand fans were waiting for the game to start and were growing increasingly irritated because it wasn't. No one could quite figure out what the holdup could possibly be since the weather was beautiful and the teams were fully warmed up. Men on the field were arguing with the umpires about something or another, and finally word began to filter out: The Elites were refusing to play the game if Josh Gibson was penciled into the Gray's lineup. After all, the Elites argued, weren't the jumpers banned from the league? A tense ten minutes passed before the Elites agreed to play the game under protest.[1]

That Sunday the Washington Elites beat the Pittsburgh Homestead Grays 8–4 to pull into the lead for the second half pennant of the Negro National League. In the second game of the doubleheader, Josh hit a home run that "sailed far over the left field wall" for one of "the longest drives seen in park history." But Josh didn't get credit for his monster shot since the second game was called in the fourth inning because of Baltimore's curfew law that "prohibit[ed] the playing of Sabbath baseball after 6 p.m."[2]

The Elites' protest was denied. With Josh officially back in the Grays' lineup, the team was transformed into a juggernaut. The Grays swept a five-game, multiple-city series against the Elites in West Virginia and Ohio: Charleston, West Virginia, 8–2; Columbus, Ohio, 7–4; Fairmont West Virginia, 8–4; and Cleveland, Ohio, 3–2 and 5–0. In the Fairmont game, Josh hit three home runs to dead center in four at bats.[3]

With Josh's bat in the lineup, the race for the Negro National League pennant ended a week before the season ended. During that 1937 season, despite taking off seven weeks to journey to the land of Trujillo, twenty-six-year-old Josh Gibson hit thirteen home runs in twenty-five games.

Two years later Walter "Big Train" Johnson, the legendary pitcher and manager of the Major League Washington Senators, saw Josh play. Big Train enthused to the *Washington Post*, "Any big league club would like to buy" Gibson for $200,000.

"He can do everything. He hits that ball a mile. And he catches so easy he might just as well be in a rocking chair. Throws like a rifle. Bill Dickey isn't as good a catcher. Too bad this Gibson is a colored fellow."[4]

• • •

Up until 1939 Josh's friends had always known him to be a happy man with a quick, deep laugh—"just an overgrown kid who did nothing but play ball and eat ice cream or go to the movies." But by 1940 bitterness began to seep in. His friends noticed that Josh "was kind of bitter with somebody, or mad with somebody, [they weren't] really sure who." They felt his harsh mood grew out of the realization "that he was never going to make the big leagues."[5]

Suddenly in the summer of 1942, thirty-one-year-old Josh began tiring easily, speaking incoherently, and often acting agitated. When Josh faced Satchel in the 1942 Negro League World Series, Satchel was in top form, but Josh had nothing. He went 2 for 13 in the series and was pulled for another catcher.[6]

Once the season ended, Josh visited his doctor, who told him to take time off to rest. Instead he played nonstop, relentlessly working to get back his old swing. Still the headaches came; the fatigue pulled him down. Yet he played through it all. Then on New Year's Day 1943, Josh lost consciousness and fell into a coma. He spent ten days in the hospital. When he finally came home, he confided to his sister Annie that he been diagnosed with a brain tumor. He told her he had refused surgery because he was sure it would turn him into a vegetable.[7]

By the late 1930s the Homestead Grays were splitting their "home" games between Griffith Stadium in Washington DC and Forbes Field in Pittsburgh. During those summers Josh began bringing Josh Jr. with him on road trips to Washington. Josh Jr. remembered that the first lesson his dad had to teach him "was that after you'd get to D.C. you'd read the signs—colored or white." Even though they played at a Major League baseball stadium, father and son were forced to stay in black-only hotels.[8]

Following the doctor's diagnosis, Josh's condition worsened. He suffered mental breakdowns on a regular basis and eventually was committed to St. Elizabeth's Hospital, a psychiatric facility in Washington DC, for ten days. Soon he sank into heavy drinking, some even thought drug use.[9] Yet he continued to play. And he continued to hit. That year he hit .474 with twelve home runs in 192 at bats.[10] By 1944 and 1945 Josh was in a state of steady physical decline. Often he would become disoriented and dizzy while chasing after high pop flies.[11]

The 1946 season kicked off with trade rumors and a report from spring training that Josh had "not fully recovered from a nervous condition."[12] On opening day Josh hit a grand slam to key a 9–8 victory over the Baltimore Elites.[13] Later that May he hit a 450-feet homer that "zoomed like a rocket over Forbes Field's left field fence" to defeat the New York Black Yankees.[14] Josh hit his final home run against the New York Cubans in late September.

By season's end, despite his heavy drinking, Josh lost weight rapidly. Friends often encountered him on the streets or in the bars of Pittsburgh holding imaginary conversations with Babe Ruth and Joe DiMaggio.[15] Then on the evening of January 19, 1947, he returned home half-drunk and went to bed complaining of a headache.[16] That night Josh died of a "stroke."[17]

Wendell Smith, the great sports editor for the *Pittsburgh Courier* eulogized Josh: "The Great Umpire has silenced the mighty bat of one of baseball's greatest sluggers of all time, Joshua (Josh) Gibson, the peer of Negro catchers, and the man whose prodigious feats at the plate have thrilled baseball fans across the Nation and on the sultry soil of Latin America for the past nineteen years. The king of sluggers is dead ... long live the king!"[18]

A large funeral was held, and Josh was buried in the Allegheny Cemetery. On a 1975 trip to Pittsburgh, Pedro "Pete" Zorilla, a Puerto Rican baseball executive who had seen Josh play, tried to visit Josh's grave to pay his respects. Soon he found himself searching among graves marked with a small round metal caps, all stamped with a number. Zorilla sought out his friend Ted Page to help him locate Josh's grave. They were able to find the grave only after locating an elderly undertaker who miraculously still had a key to the numbered graves. Upon discovering that Josh was buried in a virtually anonymous grave, the two started a fund drive to provide a proper headstone. Star Pirate first baseman Willie Stargell was the first to donate. Only after this public embarrassment did Major League Baseball agree to pay for the stone.[19]

18

The Fall of Trujillo

As the summer of 1937 turned into fall, the dictator's passion for his mistress Lina burned with ever-greater intensity. When her twenty-first birthday arrived on September 23, 1937, Trujillo's love for Lina was splashed over the front page of the capital's newspaper. There for the nation to see was an oversize picture of Queen Lina I accompanied by an anonymous poem that everyone knew had been penned by Trujillo:

> She was born a queen, not by dynastic right but by the right of beauty, and so when the chords that filled the air during her splendid reign—laughter, music, fantasy—fell silent, she still reigned with the power of that right—her beauty.
>
> There is nothing under the sun comparable to the bewitchment of her eyes—stars for the sky where the nightingale wanders giving voice to the mystery of the night. Her hands—silk, amber, perfume—have been made for the ermine of the glove and for the passion of the kiss. On her lips, whose fire evokes the pomegranate flower, lingers always her smile—irresistible seal of charm and conquest!—that is as sweet and soft as those pink and blue tints announcing the aurora.
>
> The seductive power of Anacoana, the poetess Queen of Jaragua, abides in her eyes as an immortal bewitchment, as a remote enchantment.
>
> Such is Lina: one of those beautiful women whom divinity sends to the world only rarely, so heaven's voice may come to earth and poetry sing its glory with silver trumpets.[1]

Soon thereafter at an evening party for the smart set, Queen Lina I showed off her new sparkling diamond bracelet to the U.S. ambassador's wife.[2]

• • •

In the time of Trujillo, a joke made the rounds: One day a well-fed dog strolled into Haiti. He soon came across a gaunt dog that looked sideways at his visitor and asked, "Are you mad? Why did you come to this land of hunger?" "Why did I come here," replied the Dominican dog, "why I came here to bark, to bark!"[3]

When October 1937 arrived along the Rio Masacre, the normal trickle of lean Haitians walking west across the river border back into Haiti grew to a stream. Somehow they had gleaned ominous rumors about their people in the border town of Bánica.

Two days later a great uproar took hold of Dajabón, a Dominican city and major border crossing nested along the Rio Masacre. A bustle radiated away from the Parroquia Nuestra Señora del Rosario Church, where a dance was being held that night. All day long men scurried about the city. Cars and trucks arrived at the church with *refrescos*, flowers, and decorations. A handsome podium was carted into the church. The streets were swept, beggars were shooed away, windows were washed, and Dominican flags were placed all over the city on walls, in windows, and off any existing flagpole. Above all a large portrait of President Rafael Trujillo was moved into the church, where it was placed between two large Dominican flags and rubbed until it sparkled. By midafternoon men carrying machine guns seized control of all strategic points in and around town.

Just as dusk set in, Dominicans scurried to the church from the countryside after hearing that a celebrity was coming. When night fell, the presidential motorcade pulled up to the curb. Well-armed men in crisp Guardia uniforms jumped off the running boards of the lead car and the trailing long Packard. They quickly formed a human security corridor. The soldiers saluted the president as he emerged from his car. For a passing second Trujillo looked up at the church's tiered, white-stucco bell tower; then he lowered his head and pasted a stern look on his face as he walked past the crowd into the auditorium.

People pressed at the windows to catch a glimpse of the president. "I came to the border country," he proclaimed, "to see what I could do for Dominicans living here. I found that Haitians had been stealing food and cattle from our farmers here. I found that our people would be happier if we got rid of the Haitians." He paused, then stamped his foot, raised his hand, and enunciated slowly and empathically, "I will fix that. Yesterday three hundred Haitians were killed at Bánica. This must continue."[4]

As quickly as the word spread among the Haitians living in Trujillo's country, it was beaten by the word of Trujillo. That next day soldiers aided by handpicked thugs rounded up 1,900 Haitians and corralled them in Santiago's main square, which was hedged in by government buildings. The horror lasted for hours. Soldiers brandishing machetes and clubs encircled the men, women, children, often whole families. Thugs methodically bludgeoned, clubbed, and hacked the innocents to death.[5] Despite the midday heat the nearby residents closed their shutters to muffle the cries of the doomed. As night fell, trucks piled high with corpses began leaving the square, with blood dripping from their tailgates. All that remained in the morning was a trail of blood leading to dusty roads.

That same day in the northern port city of Monte Cristi, hundreds of Haitians were herded to the docks. They were marched to the end of the harbor pier, where their hands and feet were bound. The soldiers ganged up to push them en masse into the deep waters, knowing that their corpses would be conveniently devoured by the sharks of the Sargasso Sea.[6]

Back at border crossing in Dajabón, Trujillo's troops perched by the side of the road leading to the bridge over the shallow brown water of Rio Masacre. As panic spread inland from the killings, multitudes funneled toward Dajabón on donkeys and on foot, desperate to cross the river border back into Haiti. When the first crush of Haitians arrived, they were cut down by soldiers swinging machetes. Wave after wave of Haitians were slaughtered until the arms of the soldiers grew weary. Despite strict orders against using their guns, the exhausted soldiers began firing on the fleeing Haitians with their Krag rifles.[7] In what became a relay of death, teams of soldiers carted the corpses down to the banks of the river to dump them in. In desperation the fleeing Haitians tried to cross downstream and upstream from the main road. The Dominican soldiers spread out, and moved to the banks of the river to cut down their victims on the shores. After just a few hours, the Rio Masacre was choked with the mangled, rotting corpses of Haitians and their donkeys.[8]

Like variations on a danse macabre, the slaughter played out differently in Pedenales, Jimaní, Bánica, Dajabón, Monte Cristi, Santiago, and as far away as Samaná. In urban areas the soldiers fanned out in roving bands. House-to-house searches were conducted. Any Haitians they found were ordered to immediately leave their homes, for repatriation they were told. They were transported to crudely improvised or borrowed corrals guarded by soldiers. Once the corrals were brimming with Haitians, the soldiers closed in to decapitate them with machetes. After the bodies were hauled away, dirt was spread over the ground to hide the blood. Then the corrals were again filled, and the Haitians again slaughtered. Torsos, together with severed heads, were tossed into the back of trucks that were driven to remote ravines, creeks, or, where possible, the ocean. There they dumped their bloody loads. On Trujillo's word between fifteen thousand and twenty thousand Haitians were murdered.[9]

Trujillo put a muzzle on the Dominican press. For three weeks there was no mention of the massacre. Then, on the morning of October 21, 1937, an insignificant three-inch item ran in the *New York Times* on page 17 sandwiched between much longer daily stories about a small plane crash in Salt Lake City and a political fight between the Rhode Island governor and racetrack operators. Under the headline "Haitians Reported Shot by Dominican Soldiers," the massacre was described as "a border clash . . . in which several were shot."[10] Four days later the *Times* reported, "More than 300 persons were killed. . . . The final toll would reach 1,700 dead."[11]

It took over a month after the killings for Trujillo to feel enough pressure to publically concede that something had happened. On the same day that the *New York Times* pushed the death toll to 2,700, *Listín Diario* brushed it all off as "incidents" that "are not of an international character, nor are they invested with an importance and gravity which may impair the good relations between the two neighboring Republics."[12] The following day President Roosevelt was briefed that "the total deaths might exceed 5,000."[13]

It took until early December for Haitian president Stenio Vincent, who until now had remained eerily silent, to charge that eight thousand Haitians had been victims of "mass murder."[14] The first sign that Trujillo realized a storm was brewing came a week later, when his newspapers reported that sixty farmers had been arrested for retaliating against Haitians who had plundered their fields and livestock. In lockstep Trujillo's national congress passed a resolution voicing its "solidarity and its adhesion to his [Trujillo's] international policy" concerning Haiti and for protecting "the dignity, decorum, and rights of the Dominican people."[15]

Quentin Reynolds, the thirty-five-year-old star editor of the powerful American magazine *Collier's*, was curious to discover the truth. So he caught a plane to Ciudad Trujillo to see what he could uncover.

At once President Trujillo invited the pudgy, curly-haired

Collier's editor to dine with him at one of his clubs. As Trujillo plied the editor with fine wine, Reynolds was immediately struck by Trujillo's ability to answer his toughest questions about the killings with a patient paternal smile and "apparent frankness." "The whole affair," Rafael stated smoothly, "has been overemphasized. Some Haitians crossed the border, probably to steal cattle or goats. Some Dominican farmers fought with them. Many were killed on both sides." "It is a regrettable incident," he continued, "and no one feels worse than I do about it. However, it is certainly no cause for international action."[16]

Rafael finished his argument by invoking "stand-your-ground" laws. "You see, it is like this," he argued. "A thief comes into my house and I deal with him according to my own law. There is no reason for anyone else butting in." Reynolds pressed the dictator: "But Haiti believes that the Dominican army did the killing?" "The killing," Trujillo countered with a friendly smile, "as I understand it, was done with knives and machetes. My army carries rifles and uses machine guns."[17]

"I would have believed him—anyone would have," Reynolds thought, "if I hadn't looked into the tortured eyes of mothers who had seen their families wiped out."[18]

Next the *Collier's* editor traveled to the Haitian border, where he met many of the surviving victims including Madame Telsaint Telfort. She told Reynolds that Trujillo's soldiers kept firing at her as she staggered across the river "with a bullet in her arm." Reynolds discovered that "it was a bullet from a Krag rifle. The Dominican army use[d] Krag rifles." He was sickened by the carnage. "It is easy," he thought, "to look at a bullet wound after you have seen a machete wound. Anything is easy to look at after you have seen a machete wound."[19]

The pressure mounted. The *New York Times* kept publishing; the U.S. State Department kept asking questions. Finally Trujillo's agents heard that Reynolds was about to publish a major exposé in *Collier's*. The dictator folded.

To the astonishment of his nation, on January 8, 1938, Trujillo made an address by radio, declining to run for reelection as president: "I shall begin formulating a categorical reaffirmation of my purpose previously revealed on many occasions, to relinquish official investiture in order to enjoy the peaceful rest of private live. "[20]

"Dread transformed the faces of men of industry," *Listín Diario* wrote. "The foreign colony was impressed. Anguish and intense silence drowned the hopeless cry that swelled the heart of the republic."[21]

Just as suddenly the reelection campaign, which had been up and running for nearly two years, was abandoned. Trujillo opted to install his trustworthy friend Vice President Jacinto Peynado as president. Anyone wondering how things stood needed only to stroll by President Peynado's home. Over the entrance hung a large neon sign that read, "Dios y Trujillo," "God and Trujillo."[22]

While political processes could be manipulated, nature could not. That year in Ciudad Trujillo, carnival queen Lina Lovatón bore Trujillo a daughter, whom they named Yolanda.[23] The ex-president was moved to make Lina's new baby legitimate, so he had congress immediately pass a national law to make children born out of wedlock legitimate with the proviso that the child's mother was not cheating on her husband when she conceived.[24]

A much bigger problem, however, was brewing. For months First Lady Doña María had been storming around Ciudad Trujillo, brimming over with hatred. In her mind the repercussions would be far worse than the sting of a public affair, for she believed that Lina posed a real threat to her marriage. Before long there was a failed assassination attempt on Lina with all signs pointing to the Doña. That was too much for Trujillo. He loudly let it be known that *anyone* who hurt Lina would be liquidated. Within days he sent his financial agents to Florida to quietly purchase a house for Lina. They found her a magnificent Miami mansion, which had once been owned by General Motors president Alfred Sloan. There Trujillo installed Lina with her family. Thereafter she and her family lived in safety while being provided for generously.[25]

It was no secret that the dictator and Lina remained devoted to each other to the end of their lives. Lina bore the dictator two children. And often quasi-conjugal visits were arranged in the following decades—depending on the proximity and/or the mood of the Doña—at times in secret and at times very much in the open.

After his passion for Lina had cooled down, the dictator knew no love, only lust. Cursed was the man upon whose daughter Trujillo's leer fell. The heartsick father was compelled to serve his daughter up to the dictator.

Word traveled around the capital city in the early 1950s that relations had unraveled between the Doña and her husband. Folks in the know felt sure that a divorce was in the works. The Doña began hearing this rumor all too often for her own liking. So she waited for a moment when she was alone with her husband "in the privacy of the nuptial chamber." Pulling a gun on her husband, she crisply announced she would "put a hole in him" if he divorced her. Trujillo put aside his divorce plans. Using his many available forms of persuasion, he cajoled the Vatican into issuing a papal dispensation to remarry the Doña in a Catholic Church in 1955. Thus the Doña and the dictator achieved conjugal peace.[26]

• • •

Dominicans never gave up their fight for freedom. Much of their struggle is hard to document as Trujillo was every bit as effective at wiping out evidence of opposition as he was at wiping out the opposition. Many, like the gifted writer Juan Bosch, felt they had no choice but to flee into exile and to resist from abroad. Others stayed at home to resist. There were waves of bombings of schools and public buildings in Santiago in the 1930s and 1940s.[27] Yet as Trujillo tightened his grip on all aspects of Dominican society, it became nearly impossible to operate a broadly organized resistance movement. Conspiracies had to remain compact. As the years passed, most of the efforts to oust Trujillo took the form of assassination plots or offshore invasions. In May 1956 a small group of conspirators wired explosives under a church in Moca, which Trujillo was slated to dedicate. Only days before the event, an informer turned in the conspirators. The church dedication went off as scheduled.[28]

By the 1950s several large anti-Trujillo organizations led by exiled Dominicans took root in New York City and San Juan, Puerto Rico. Juan Bosch's Partido Revolucionario Dominicano (PRD) was the most effective of these groups, organizing everything from picket lines at the Dominican Embassy to political rallies and public information campaigns to open meetings.

However, it was the exiled Jesús de Galíndez Suárez who came to occupy a special place of hatred in Rafael Trujillo's heart. Galíndez was a Basque nationalist who had fled to Ciudad Trujillo at the end of the Spanish Civil War. He was soon disgusted by Trujillo's dictatorship and left for New York City. There Galíndez became a lecturer in international law at Columbia University. Overnight he became one of the key authorities on Trujillo's government. At the time it became widely known that he was completing a scathing indictment of Trujillo as his doctoral thesis.

On a calm spring evening in 1956, Galíndez wrapped up his lecture at Columbia's Fayerweather Hall. He accepted a ride from one of his students to the subway station at the corner of Fifty-Seventh and Eighth Avenue. He thanked her, waved good-bye, and then entered the New York subway system, where he disappeared.[29] Bosch's PRD quickly charged that Trujillo was behind the professor's disappearance. His actions jumped the case to the status of a cause célèbre for the American and international press. News organizations in the late 1950s closely followed all the new developments in the Galíndez case like an unfolding murder mystery. For Trujillo this had the painful effect of shining an international light into the darkest corners of his dictatorship.

The generation of Dominicans who came of age in the late 1950s thirsted for the liberty that their parents had given up on. They called their movement to overthrow the dictator Catorce de Junio or 1J4.[30] Once Trujillo's agents caught wind of their conspiracy, they began mass roundups, jailing, and torturing of the conspirators. Three of the 1J4 leaders were married to three Mirabal sisters—Dr. Minerva Mirabal de Tavárez, María Teresa Mirabal de Guzmán, and Patria Mirabal de González. Each of the sisters had been jailed and tortured early in 1960 for their associations with 1J4. Yet even in the face of grave danger, they continued to stand by their husbands. They repeatedly embarrassed the dictator by visiting their husbands in jail. Trujillo grew so personally incensed at the brazen defiance by the sisters that, in a fit of rage, he ordered their assassination by his secret police.

Trujillo's secret police dangled the promise of a visit with their husbands to lure the sisters into a trap. On their way to see their husbands, Trujillo's men waylaid the sisters' car, dragged them into a sugarcane field, and clubbed them to death. Their corpses were placed back inside their car and driven up a winding mountain road near Santiago, where it was pushed off a high cliff. Unfortunately for Trujillo, his bloody farce fooled no one. From that day, November 25, 1960, a visceral hatred of his regime pervaded the country.

On May 30, 1961, after the breeze from the Caribbean began reversing direction and the air had cooled, Trujillo took his daily walk along El Malecón. The dictator was now an old man. As he aged, he was often plagued by fits of incontinence, and he became so anxious about his darkening complexion that he began caking his face with pale foundation and powder before public appearances.

Once the breeze fully flipped, Trujillo finished his afternoon *paseo* along El Malecón. He returned promptly to his office to wrap up lingering administrative chores. Chores completed, he summoned his driver, Zacharias, to take him to visit his daughter Angelina. It wasn't until about 10:00 p.m. that he ordered Zacharias to drive him to his estate just outside San Cristobal so he could relax in the arms of his young concubine.

The road to San Cristobal originated at Trujillo's quarter-sized Washington Monument. Zacharias glided onto this road in their light-blue 1957 Chevrolet Bel Air, adorned with a chrome swan hood ornament and long, sleek chrome horns mounted on the passenger-side fender. He slowly eased the car up to sixty miles per hour as they hit the open road. Suddenly their rear windshield exploded. Blood gushed from under the dictator's left armpit. "Coño [cunt]," Trujillo snarled. "I've been hit."[31] Zacharias screeched their car to a halt in the middle of the highway. An angry Trujillo grabbed his revolver. In a fraction of a second, before Zacharias could stop him, Trujillo staggered out of the rear passenger door to take revenge. With cold purpose the assassins walked toward the dictator and unloaded their powerful weapons into him. Trujillo's revolver fired a single shot in the air as he fell to his knees. His face pitched forward onto the still-warm pavement.

The three assassins roughly grabbed the corpse. They hauled it to their car and pitched it into the trunk. In the middle of the road lay Trujillo's bloody dental bridge.

Joy swept the populace:

Ay, Maria, Maria, Maria
Sing and don't cry
Because singing you make

Honey, the heart happy

They've killed Chapita
On the highway
They've killed Chapita
On the highway

Let's shout
Let's shout
In this way
They've killed Chapita
And won't let me see

—Popular Dominican merengue from December 1961

Rafael Trujillo habitually consulted brujos possessing the power of divination.[32] Before he seized power, a famed brujo had prophesized that he would be swept into power by a hurricane and out by one.[33] This prophecy caused Trujillo to obsessively track hurricanes during his thirty years in power. Hurricane Frances made landfall near Cape Cana of the Dominican Republic in early October 1961; six weeks later Trujillo's family was forced into permanent exile off the island.

• • •

Trujillo thought the young man was smart. Smart was trouble. So he sent twenty-five-year-old Juan Bosch to jail—just to think things over. He let a few months go by. When the young writer was released, he was surprised to learn that he had been appointed director of government statistics. Shortly thereafter Trujillo dropped by on Bosch unannounced to let him know that he had been appointed "chief of journalism and literature." Just as the meeting was ending, Trujillo dropped a by-the-way request that Bosch write a series of laudatory essays on the regime. Before the end of 1937, Bosch was growing increasingly troubled by events: Trujillo's phony reelection campaign, his jailing of all dissidents, his grabbing of all national economic assets for his own benefit. So sickened was Bosch by the Haitian massacre that he left for Puerto Rico.[34]

For decades Bosch lived in exile, making a living by publishing short stories, essays, and novels. At first he thought of himself as an artist who was above politics. It took a few years of living among Dominican exiles in Cuba to become convinced that political action was an imperative. There he founded the PRD in 1939. Bosch's group quickly became the loudest voice against Trujillo.

With Trujillo dead in 1961, Bosch returned to the Dominican Republic to establish a new constitution. When free elections were finally called in 1962, Bosch ran for president of the republic. He was a striking man of natural charisma who looked into people's eyes with his piercing blue irises, so large they spilled far under his eyelids. Entering a room he wore a serious near-frown that easily turned into a laugh, one that seemed to lower his black-rimmed glasses and wrinkle his high forehead. His deep intellect, in tandem with his facile grasp of language, made Bosch a spellbinding orator. As he spoke of his plans for long-needed reform, his broad mouth set off against a square jaw and high, rectangular forehead added determination to his words.

Election Day, Thursday, December 20, 1962, marked the first free, honest election in the Dominican Republic since 1924. A holiday was declared. "Men and women," the *New York Times* wrote, "dressed in their finery to stand in the long queues stretching in front of schools, public buildings and hotels when the polling places were installed." "They voted," the *Times* reported, "in a mood that combined solemnity, gaiety and some bewilderment over the intricacies of a process that was virtually unknown here even to the generation that is now in middle age."[35]

To the surprise of all observers, Juan Bosch's PRD swept to victory in a landslide, tallying 59.5 percent of the vote despite running in a field of five candidates.

It was February 1963 when Bosch rose to take the oath of office as president. Standing nearby, smiling and glad-handing was American vice president Lyndon Johnson. In his inaugural speech Bosch urged long-overdue social and economic reforms for the peasants and urban poor. It was time, Bosch insisted, to give the people of the Dominican Republic "a place in the sun among advanced nations of the Americas."[36]

President Bosch only made it to September. The military, the economic elites, and the Catholic Church banded together to oust the reformer. A triumvirate composed of rightest business and military interests tore up the new constitutions and seized power.[37]

• • •

Finally, on April 25, 1965, civil war broke out in Santo Domingo between Bosch's followers, known as "Constitutionalists," and Trujillo's old army, called "Loyalists." After a few days of fighting, it was clear that the Bosch Constitutionalist forces were on the verge of victory. In full panic President Lyndon Johnson sent in the marines. That evening he went on national television in the United States and lied, offering as his excuse the need to protect American citizens: "Let me also make clear tonight that we support no single man or any single group of men in the Dominican Republic. Our goal is a simple one. We are there to save the lives of our citizens and to save the lives of all people."[38]

Johnson left out the critical fact. When the marines landed, they sided with Trujillo's old army.[39] In fact they saved it from imminent defeat. As negotiations over a truce and new elections dragged on for months, the Americans got busy reconstituting, resupplying, and even paying the salaries of Trujillo's old army.[40]

Election Day arrived on Saturday, January 1, 1966. Bosch faced off against Trujillo's ex-puppet president Joaquín Balaguer. Balaguer's method for winning the election was simple. Tru-

jillo's freshly reconstituted army was given the green light
to unleash a reign of terror to crush any existing or nascent
opposition; the army made it known to Bosch that if he ven-
tured out of his home to campaign he would be killed.[41] Once
Balaguer won the rigged election, he sicced Trujillo's old army
on Bosch's supporters; at least 350 of them were killed in the
first six months of 1966.[42]

• • •

Dr. Jose Enrique Aybar stayed on the island after Trujillo's family fled. For a time he was a pariah. But his fortunes turned when
Bosch was forced out of power by a military coup. On the day that
the U.S. Marines spread out across Ciudad Trujillo, they seized
houses at key intersections to secure their positions. Sweeping
west the soldiers came to Calle Dr. Delgado. It was clear to them
that the house at the corner of San Juan Bosco was ideal for their
purposes. The marines surrounded the house and demanded
that the residents come out with their hands above their heads.
Out charged a small gray-haired man brandishing a revolver.
The squad of marines unloaded their guns into the little man,
who, it turned out, had been an ally: Dr. Jose Enrique Aybar.[43]

Trujillo's gang-member friend, Miguel Ángel Paulino, had
slowly ascended to the rank of general under Trujillo. When
the Trujillos fled, Paulino fled too. Only after the military coup
ousted Bosch did General Paulino return to the country. Just
a few years later, in January 1968, he was gunned down on the
streets of Santo Domingo by a jealous musician.[44]

• • •

Thirty-seven years after the assassinations of the Mirabal sisters, a
crowd gathered at the Trujillo Obelisk. Its white surface had been
painted over with colorful larger-than-life images of the three sisters.[45] At the rededication of this marble monument, the Dominican poet Carmen Sanchez read her poem "Danza de eternidad."[46]

19

The Persevering Paige

The black overhead fans did the best they could on a late afternoon in June to disperse the hot, grimy Pittsburgh air. Downing a cold, strong drink did a far better job. Gus Greenlee sat in Club Crawford taking the liquid approach. It was late afternoon, when there was usually a lull between the reports from the men of his numbers racket and his Crawford Grill beginning to fill with customers. Gus became lost in thought.

That sonuvabitch Satch—Gus should have known that he would run off. He had done it to him twice already. Gus had thrown Satch the biggest party ever when he married Janet, and he had acted like it was nothing and taken off to some rich white guy in North Dakota. Gus should never have taken him back, but he had, and, sure enough, off he went again. Gus should have remembered: get good at something, and everyone wants your money. The whole damn team had taken off after Satch, along with the goddamn politicians, police, do-gooders, girlfriends— hell, he wasn't even sure they were really girlfriends, should just call 'em moneyfriends. When you're poor, you don't have many friends or even many folks wanting to be your friend. You have "friends" who up and vanish into thin air the second your tire hits a rock. When you have money, well, you have "friends" all right, always looking for something—"Hey Gus, how about money for that dress. Oh and I saw this nice necklace in the window downtown. I'm a little behind on rent—you can understand." Goddamn lawyers were just like those ballplayers and girlfriends. Once you start paying them, they never stop asking.

It is clear that Gus called Commissioner Morton on the telephone and demanded that the players be banned from organized baseball for one year and fined. He even went so far as
to demand indictments.[1]

Throughout spring and into the summer, Gus, who wore
both the hat of team owner and that of league president, roared
at the State Department about the Dominicans while having
his talented publicist, John Clark, plant negative stories about
Trujillo in the American press. "IT'S BLACK MAGIC!" screamed
a *Chicago Daily Tribune* headline. "DICTATOR STEALS 17 BALL
PLAYERS." The paper even hyperventilated that "the peace of
nations [was] at issue." "The dictator-president," it proclaimed,
"will stop at nothing to attain diamond supremacy for his republic, it is said, and when a visiting team came to Ciudad Trujillo [Guess who the capital's named after] he even put them
up in the palace."[2]

July came. Gus still believed reports from his expensive lawyers that the State Department was on the verge of mandat-
ing the return of the jumpers—fully unaware that Paige and
his fellow Negro League jumpers were playing their last few
games on the island.[3] As Greenlee raged at Trujillo, his Pittsburgh Crawfords floundered. After finishing first the previous
year, his beloved team had fallen to fifth place out of six teams
with a 12-16 record.

• • •

Satchel was in the money. Years later he told the tall tale that
he had split Trujillo's $30,000 with the other jumpers. It wasn't
so. When Satchel took the $30,000 from the Dominicans, Cy
Perkins was the only American player to jump with him out of
New Orleans. Jabbo Andrews was already down there. Harry
Williams, Leroy Matlock, Cool Papa Bell, Sammy Bankhead,

and Schoolboy Griffith were late-season signings by Aybar. They traveled down to the Dominican Republic a month after Satchel and Cy. Aybar, in a fit of defensive pique, shed light on his own financial arrangements when he published what he paid the other players—Josh $2,200, everyone else $1,500.[4] It's most likely that Satchel gave Cy $3,000 and kept the remaining $27,000 for himself.

Splits aside, all the jumpers left the Dominican Republic with pockets full of money, fully physically spent from days of celebrating after Paulino released them from his *estricto control*. The only player missing for the trip back was the lovestruck pitcher Bert Hunter, who stayed behind to settle on the island with his Dominican sweetheart. Josh left with the other jumpers but headed back to Pittsburgh to make good on his promise to finish out the season with the Homestead Grays.

Without missing a beat, Satchel and the jumpers put on Trujillo's fancy uniforms and announced the creation of an "All-Star" team to barnstorm across America for the remainder of 1937 as the Ciudad Trujillo All-Stars. It was surreal sight: banned black ballplayers barnstorming across America wearing uniforms emblazoned across the chest with "C. Trujillo"—all the while laughing in Gus Greenlee's face.

To book their games Satchel cut a deal with midwestern sports promoter Ray Doan. Ray was widely known as a promotional wizard who handled all of Dizzy Dean's off-season appearances. Satchel knew Ray as a master at raising a crowd; among Ray's favorite tricks was presenting softball games in which the players were tethered to goats. Ciudad Trujillo All-Stars bookings were right in Ray's wheelhouse.

Shortly after returning to the United States, Satchel's Ciudad Trujillo team traveled to Denver to play in the Denver Post Tournament, known in those days as the Little World Series. Ciudad Trujillo made headlines by sweeping to victory and winning the $5,000 prize.[5] Ciudad Trujillo then hopped on a bus and slowly wound its way east. When the team rolled into Lincoln, Nebraska, the *Evening Journal* was so fooled by the team's name that it ran a story under the headline "PRESIDENT OF SANTO DOMINGO HIRES TEAM TO PLAY FOR HIS COUNTRY."[6] Next stop was Chicago, where the team whipped the Duffy Florals in a pair of Sunday games.[7] Ciudad Trujillo then went on to Kansas City to play the Monarchs. Next stop was Cleveland for a game against the New York Cubans.

Late September brought Ciudad Trujillo to New York City, where the team played at the Polo Grounds. For the season finale Satchel pitched a 9 to 4 victory over the Negro National League Stars before thirty thousand fans at Yankee Stadium.[8] As Satchel's Ciudad Trujillo team played in New York, Yankee star Joe DiMaggio praised him in the newspapers as "the best pitcher" he had ever faced.[9]

Just six days later, the World Series pitting the Giants against the Yankees opened at Yankee Stadium. For their Game One starter, the Giants ran out thirty-three-year-old Carl Hubbell. King Carl was knocked out of the game in the sixth by the young Yankees, led by twenty-one-year-old Joe DiMaggio. The Yankees whipped the Giants four games to one by scoring an average of over 5½ runs per game.

Satchel sent a telegram to Giants manager Bill Terry suggesting that "the disaster might have been averted by using 'Ethiopian' pitchers." Then the weekly *Afro-American* ran a large cartoon on its sports page under the title "TRY COLORED PITCHERS" picturing DiMaggio knocking the over-the-hill Hubbell silly with line drives off his bat. The paper's editorial went far beyond Satchel's hint that the Giants could have improved their lineup by including black players, writing that the Yankees had no right to be considered world champions; after all "nobody knows whether they could lick such teams as the Homestead Grays, Washington Elites or even Paige's team."[10]

Everyone knew that baseball commissioner Kenesaw Mountain Landis, who hailed from a city right over the border from Kentucky, was immovable on the race question—so immovable that the black press began calling him "the Great White Father." In the wake of the 1937 World Series, the *Afro-American* made a direct appeal to Landis, arguing that not until the Majors were "freed from the stigma of the color bar" could they rightly be considered "the picture of American democracy, fair play and good sportsmanship."[11] Landis simply ignored the editorial.

After the end of the 1937 World Series, even the *New York Daily News* made a pitch for ending the Major League's color bar: "Certainly colored players could play at the Stadium or Polo Grounds without starting race riots, though it may do well to go easy in, say, Washington. We think the New York teams ought to take the lead in erasing this unjust and foolish remnant of the color line in American sports."[12] Landis simply ignored that editorial too.

It took until 1942 for the heat generated by Wendell Smith, the brilliant sports editor of the *Pittsburgh Courier*, to force Landis to respond directly. "There is no rule, formal or informal, or any understanding—unwritten, subterranean, or sub-anything—against the hiring of Negro players by the teams of organized ball," Landis pompously huffed.[13] "The statement of the high commissioner is just a lot of words . . . just another case of hypocritical buck passing," rebutted the *Los Angeles News*.[14]

Spring training in 1938 approached. Having no answer for the audacious Satchel and the jumpers, the Negro League owners dropped their bans and lowered their fines. Satchel found that the owners who had "been saying [he] was killing them and busting up their clubs" were now smiling at him "real pretty."[15] He joked that the owners had "developed the shortest memories you ever saw anywhere around about [him] jumping the Crawfords."[16] Hardly skipping a beat, Greenlee stepped first in line to re-sign Satchel for the 1938 season.

Back and forth it went between Gus and Satchel in the black

press during the spring of 1938. Satchel fired the first shot by threatening to organize his own team to tour Latin America unless the league began paying players a decent wage. He asked, "How can we continue to exist on the measly hand-out they give us?"[17] Greenlee shot back, stating, "[If they] refuse to sign under the conditions proposed, they can go right on back to Santo Domingo."[18]

Gus's publicity arm talked the *Afro-American* newspaper into running a cartoon under the title "THE PRODIGAL SON RETURNS" picturing Gus smiling as he paternalistically embraces Josh and Satchel. Gus announced that he was generously offering Satchel $350 a month to pitch for the Crawfords. Satchel shot back that he "wouldn't throw ice cubes for that kind of money."[19] In response Gus planted a column that mocked Satchel's demands by claiming age had caught up with him—"he wasn't the pitcher he once was." Satchel retorted that he was sitting things out on Joe DiMaggio's advice to "keep holding out until [he got] results."[20]

Gus cracked. He sold Satchel's contract to the Newark Eagles for $5,000 with the proviso that he would be paid when Satchel reported to the team. Satchel bailed. He signed a far more lucrative deal to play for the Mexico City baseball team Agrario. Gus went apoplectic. The Mexico signing had made his $5,000 contract worthless.

Bursting with impotent rage, Gus had the Negro National League pass a rule to "bar Satchell Paige forever from organized baseball" and one forbidding league teams from playing "any team with which Paige [was] connected" or "in any park where he appear[ed]."[21] The only person level-headed enough to understand the truth of it all was Homestead Grays owner Cum Posey, who remarked, "Did you read that Mr. Satchell Paige was tossed out of organized baseball? That is also hooey. Satchell will come back when he feels like it, and the League members will be glad to have him in the League."[22]

In truth Satchel's trip to Mexico was as much to get away from his new wife, Janet, as to make more money. Janet had caught Satchel's eye while she was waitressing for Gus Greenlee at the Crawford Grill. That was in 1931, when Satchel had first arrived in Pittsburgh. After weeks of small talk that turned into flirting, it became clear that Janet was Satchel's favorite girl. Her instincts told her that Satchel was not a man to be pinned down easily. So she went out of her way to feign only a casual interest; when she deigned to date him, she took things slow. Once she had Satchel hooked, she pounced, demanding a date for the wedding. Cornered Satchel agreed to October 26, 1934.

Gus played host, shutting down the Crawford Grill to throw a wedding with a lavish reception for the couple. That afternoon the "who's who" of black Pittsburgh poured into the grill. Satchel's favorite friend, the famous tap dancer Bojangles Robinson, served as his best man. Of course Gus had an ulterior motive: now that Satchel was getting tied down with a woman, he felt the timing was perfect to tie him down with a long-term contract. Gus put Janet in Satchel's ear to push for an agreement before the wedding. He patiently waited for the party to reach a high pitch. Then clinking his glass with a silver fork, Gus hushed the crowd. "Satchel won't be leaving us," he bellowed. "I've got a new contract here for him."[23] Janet stood behind the two with a big smile on her face as Satchel signed the two-year deal to toasts and applause.

The year 1934 went smoothly for Satchel, Gus, and Janet; 1935 was another matter altogether. Life as a newlywed was far more expensive than Satchel had imagined. One spring afternoon he marched into Gus's office to demand a raise on the contract he had just signed. Gus was speechless. He turned red and spluttered in anger as he kicked Satchel out of his office. Satchel stormed home and furiously began packing his belongings to leave Pittsburgh. After he had cooled down, it dawned on him that he had nowhere to go.

Only a few weeks later, a sports agent representing a semi-pro team from Bismarck, North Dakota, contacted Satchel to find out if he was ready to play for a team paying far more money than Gus. He was ready. Janet pursed her lips when he told her the news, but she reluctantly packed their belongings. They jumped into Satchel's long car and drove the 1,375 miles west to Bismarck, North Dakota. As they passed the Bismarck city limits, they slowed down to crane their necks so they could find a place to live. Driving from "for rent" sign to "for rent" sign, the couple stopped and knocked on the doors. They found the people to be supremely polite. It just so happened that every posting was incorrect. Every house with a "for rent" sign in Bismarck had just been rented—right before they got there. It turned out the only place the newlyweds could rent was an old railroad freight car that had been converted into a bunk car for work gangs. It sat on an abandoned sidetrack at the edge of town.

Stability for Janet and Gus returned in 1936. Gus and Satchel made up. Satchel was once again pitching for the Pittsburgh Crawfords, holding court at the Crawford Grill, and mostly staying home. Then in 1937 the stability that Janet had longed for was once again shattered by Satchel's unpredictable jump to the Dominican Republic. Mexico in 1938 was the end of the road.

By 1938 Satchel had played in Venezuela, Cuba, and the Dominican Republic, so Mexico didn't seem to pose any special challenge. Yet from the day he arrived, Mexico didn't agree with Satchel. He found the heat and the high altitude draining, while the spicy food kick-started his stomach miseries. It seemed that everything he ate in Mexico ended up "smacking one another and burning up [his] insides."[24]

Under Mexico's September heat, Satchel once again faced off against the great Martín Dihigo. Their first meeting came on September 5, 1938, with Dihigo pitching for the Veracruz Águila, Satchel for the Mexico City Agrario. As hard as Satchel tried to mask his sore right arm, it was apparent from the start that his high velocity was gone. Using his great control, he threw curves and trick pitches often with a submarine motion. Dihigo with his high velocity and sharp curve piled up the strikeouts.

After seven innings the tightly pitched game was knotted up 1–1. Satchel, drained by the heat, was pulled for a pinch hitter. Cuban Ramon Bragaña was given the ball to pitch the eighth and ninth for Satchel's team. Popeye Salvatierra got Dihigo's team going in the top of the ninth with a base hit to left. Dihigo walked to the plate waving a bat. He clubbed his fellow Cuban's offering over the left-field fence and into a distant meadow to provide the margin for a 3–1 victory.[25]

Satchel and Dihigo met for the last time at the baseball stadium in Mexico City on September 18, 1938. Satchel stepped onto the mound, praying that he would be able to pitch through the growing pain in his right arm. Dihigo, who often hit well against Satchel, went 6 for 6 with a home run, an extra base hit, and four singles. It marked the first time in Mexican League history that the feat had been accomplished. Satchel had nothing on this day. He was mercilessly beat down 10–3 by Dihigo's team.[26] Mexico City's newspapers branded Paige "the failure of the year" and flatly stated that it appeared he could no longer pitch effectively.[27]

Satchel had pitched through pain before, but nothing like this. After the loss he retreated to his hotel room, where he limply flopped onto his bed. He stared up at the ceiling of his room, praying that the pain would pass, trying to get his mind on other things. He tried and tried, but the biting pain deep in his arm kept grabbing back his attention.

Satchel just couldn't believe that didn't have it in him to make a comeback. After all he had been before—real sore—but, damn, never like this. He didn't know why Janet was calling so damn much for; the poor amigo downstairs at the desk had a whole pile of paper with her name and number on it.

He didn't know what had happened between him and Janet. They had been real close and then, bang, they weren't. She just never got over that summer in North Dakota. Well, it hadn't been his idea to live in a boxcar, but who got the blame? Not the white folks who wouldn't rent to them—no way; no, it always came down to old Satch. That stint in North Dakota was the one time he should have left her behind for sure. But he had thought it might be kind of nice, with farm folk and everyone all polite—not to mention that fat rich guy with all those brand new Chryslers. He should never have gone through with it. He had known it wasn't right but was just too far down the tracks to stop it—Gus with the big party, big talk, contract an all. Damn, he should have known. He had spent plenty of time telling Janet that he needed to keep moving and she kept saying, "It'll be all right, honey." He had just known, though, that it wouldn't. Janet wanted a man who ran a hardware store or something like that where he came home every night at the same time, a man with a regular paycheck. She didn't really want a husband with a lot of fancy stuff, just someone who sat down, ate dinner, chatted about all the small stuff that happened that day—even if it wasn't much—but regular.

Satchel finally gave up on talking himself through the pain and drank himself to sleep with a bottle of tequila. He fell asleep that night soaked in sweat, hoping it was not true or at least it would a little better in the morning. Or better yet maybe he would wake and discover that it had never even happened. He woke, his head throbbing, with the sun high in the sky. His arm was stiff, but the searing pain was gone. It had to be better, he thought. But when Satchel tried to lift his magic right arm, it just hung at his side, numb and useless.

Satchel dragged his lifeless arm all over Mexico City to specialist after specialist but received nothing but grim opinions. The consensus among the doctors was that he would never pitch again. Satchel's contract in Mexico only paid for the number of games he pitched. Since he couldn't pitch, he couldn't earn money, and it made no sense for him to stay in Mexico. The two things he knew for sure were that doors would be slammed in his face if he ever called on Janet or Gus.

Days passed, yet he still couldn't lift his right arm above his head. It hurt so bad he could barely dress. When he did dress, he became drenched in sweat from the pain and effort. Forget about an undershirt. The pain finally turned into numbness; it felt like something inside had been pinched off.

Satchel dragged himself back to Pittsburgh, where he holed up in a hotel room. He spent days just looking at the ceiling, knowing for certain that he was headed back to Mobile, poverty, and nobody-ness. Knowing his fame would evaporate. Knowing that all the stars, the movie actors, the famous boxers, the politicians he hobnobbed with would instantly forget he ever existed.

With the last of Satchel's cash gone, he drove from pawnshop to pawnshop hawking his prized possessions. He started with his less favorite suits and moved on to the fishing rods. The last to go were his guns. "Mr. Pawnshop," Satchel kept thinking, "must have thought I was a burglar the way I kept coming back to see him with another shotgun or another suit."[28]

In no time the word spread like venom through baseball circles that Satchel was back from Mexico with a dead arm. In fits and starts he gingerly put out feelers for a job. After all, he thought, his name would still draw fans—he could play first base while his arm healed—or he could coach. But they all said the same thing: "Remember when you let us down in 1935— oh and how about 1937 and 1938. So now you expect us to take care of you?" In an act of cruelty, the Newark Eagles, who held Satchel's contract, released a statement to the black press that generated the headline: "SATCHEL PAIGE 'NOT WANTED'"[29]

Days turned into weeks, which became months, and still nobody called. No matter how hard Satchel tried, his thoughts always circled back to the same thing: with his arm gone he was a nobody, no different from the nobody he had been as a kid in Mobile Alabama, just another black man in white America looking for his next meal.

During his struggles Satchel was haunted by the memory of the time when a group of his childhood friends from Mobile, Alabama, dropped by a fancy New York nightclub to say hello. He had ducked out the back to avoid them. As he sat on his bed thinking about his future, he came to realize "it was a mighty little man who did things that way."[30]

The year 1939 came. Satchel was down to his last few dollars when his phone rang. "This is Satch," he answered. "Satch, this is J. L. Wilkinson. I own the Kansas City Monarchs. Remember me?" "Satchel, Tom Baird, my partner, and I just got your contract from Newark," Wilkinson continued. "When can you report to Kansas City?"[31]

Without missing a beat, Satchel replied that he could be there tomorrow. J.L. told him next week would be just fine. When the call was over, Satchel sat on his bed holding the receiver, staring at it in disbelief with bright eyes and a smile on his face for the first time in months.

When Satchel finally pulled into Kansas City, he was surprised to learn that Wilkinson had gone through all the trouble to sign him just to play on the traveling B squad. J.L. told him, "Well Satch, we figure your name will draw in some fans, and well, we just thought you needed a hand right now."[32]

Satchel joined the Monarch's developmental squad, which was an odd amalgamation of prospects and has-beens. They played in any small town within a swath of territory that ran from the Deep South through the cowboy states and up into Canada. J.L. put Satchel under the nurturing eyes of Walter "Newt" Joseph, a wise, kind-faced black coach from Birmingham, Alabama, who had learned at the feet of the legendary Rube Foster. Newt had been the Monarch's third baseman for years. When his playing days were over, J.L. kept him on as a trusted member of his organization. Newt was infamous for his knack at stealing signs from opposing teams.

That April spring training for the Traveling Monarchs got under way in New Orleans. There Satchel heard the familiar sounds of "Steal away, steal away, steal away home to Jesus" at a wake in the distance. After a time he heard the funeral procession winding through the streets, with the approaching strains of "Flee as a Bird to the Mountains" turning into the high-spirited jazz chorus "Didn't he ramble?"[33] Satchel visited his old haunts, yet with a tinge of sadness. The Traveling Monarchs tuned up by playing against the Pittsburgh Homestead Grays and the New Orleans Crescent Stars.[34] Wilkinson's publicists began billing the team as "Paige's All-Stars" to build attendance.

They broke camp to travel on to Galveston, Texas, then on to Paris, where the Monarchs beat the local team while Satchel stood in as third-base coach.[35] June brought them to Chicago; Black River Falls and Milwaukee, Wisconsin; Peoria, Illinois; and Helena, Montana. As spring turned to summer, Satchel slid into a deep despair. It got so bad, he told Newt that he wanted to stop throwing. "Keep throwing," Newt advised. "What difference does it make? The fans still come out when we advertise that you'll throw. And those fans mean money in our pockets."[36]

Advertise Satchel they did:

Chanute City Team

vs.

Satchel Paige
All Star Colored Team

Come out and see Satchel Paige, fastest colored speed ball pitcher of today. Has defeated such pitchers as Dizzy Dean, Paul Dean, Schoolboy Rowe, and other major league pitchers.

Admission: Men 35¢; Ladies 25¢, Children under 12, 10¢[37]

The Monarchs reached Canada near the end of June. Newt told Satchel to warm up; he would be starting the game. Satchel slid on his glove and wandered down the sidelines to the warmup mound. That familiar sick feeling crept into his stomach as he picked up a ball, knowing the stabbing pain in his right arm would begin welling up "enough to like to kill [him]." The pain usually stopped only after he threw enough to make his arm go numb. Satchel winced in anticipation. He softly tossed the ball. No pain. He threw harder. No pain. He added a little bit more with each pitch, shaking his head in disbelief. The pain was gone. Newt came running to see what all the excitement was about. When Satchel finished up, Newt put his arm around him like a father. Satchel looked down. Tears streamed down Newt's cheeks. Together they cried.[38]

That day Satchel took the mound in Winnipeg, Canada. The local newspaper reported that fans who "remembered him of previous seasons, fast and full of fire and fun" were surprised to see "the famous negro's speed and control [reduced] to almost average proportions." And when Satchel failed to come out to pitch in the fourth inning, "he was jibbed by the fans."[39] Satchel and Newt didn't mind those jibes a bit. Of course he didn't have his old velocity back, but it would be coming. After the game they rushed back to their hotel to call J.L. to let him in on the big news. J.L. calmly urged Satchel to take things slowly with his arm because they wanted him "to join the real Monarchs for next year."[40]

Satchel's arm kept improving. On June 25 he pitched nine innings to shut out the House of David in Bismarck, North Dakota. His arm was not fully back as "he staged a halfway sitdown strike while taking some nine minutes to pitch the five balls he threw in the last half of the ninth inning."[41] A few days later it was reported in Billings, Montana, that he was unable to pitch due to a "lame arm."[42]

On July 30, he pitched in Reno, Nevada. The sportswriter

for the *Nevada State Journal* witnessed Satchel hold the Royals "spellbound" using his "deceptive slow ball, smoking fast one, wide-breaking curve and dipping downer."[43] Satchel's arm was back. He could once again throw his "smoking fast one." Only now he mixed in curves, drops, and change-ups.

The following year Satchel pitched for the "real" Monarchs. They won the 1940 Negro American League Pennant. In 1941 a fully recovered Satchel went 6-0. The following year he went 6-4 in the regular season and pitched in all four games of the Negro World Series. The Monarchs swept to the title four games to zero over the Pittsburgh Homestead Grays. A young second baseman from California named Jackie Robinson played with Satchel on those 1945 Monarchs. In 1946 Satchel went 5-1 with forty-nine strikeouts in fifty innings.

Eventually Satchel settled down in Kansas City. One night early in the 1942 season, he sighted a pretty young woman working the drugstore counter. With his camera dangling around his neck, he sauntered in to ask the young lady for some film. It hurt his feelings she didn't recognize him, didn't fuss over the famous Satchel Paige. So "like some kind of registered fool," he called the manager over to complain that she had been rude. The manager offered to fire her on the spot to which Satchel magnanimously replied, "No need to do that. All I want is the next time I come in she'll know how to conduct herself."[44]

Satchel felt so terrible about how badly he had treated this woman that he returned every day for the next week to "smooth things out." He did such a great job in the smoothing department that before long they were dating, then romancing. In 1947 they married. Lahoma Brown became Mrs. Lahoma Paige. They moved into a big brick house on Twenty-Sixth Street, where they raised five daughters and a son.

Satchel Paige had found a home in Kansas City. In J. L. Wilkinson he had found a generous, understanding team owner. In

Lahoma he had found love and family. But Lahoma never forgot that introduction. Satchel always knew it was "one of the dumbest things" he had ever said. Lahoma was no pushover. "Don't you think," Satchel would always comment with a laugh, that "Lahoma didn't play that one back to me."[45]

• • •

The man the black press called the Great White Father died on November 25, 1944. With his firm grip now off the door, which he had held so firmly shut against blacks, it suddenly opened. Brooklyn Dodgers general manager Branch Rickey made the first move. Just nine months after Landis's death, Rickey signed Kansas City Monarchs shortstop Jackie Robinson to a Minor League contract. Robinson reported to the Dodgers' Montreal Royals for the 1946 season. As a Royal Robinson ended the season as batting champion and led his team to a league title.

However, Rickey flatly refused to compensate J.L.'s Monarchs for the signing of Jackie Robinson. "There is no Negro league as such," he proclaimed from his high moral perch. "Negro baseball is in the zone of a racket and there is no Negro circuit that could be admitted to organized baseball."[46] Of all the Negro League owners, the Monarch's J. L. Wilkinson was hit the hardest by the uncompensated raids on the Negro Leagues by Rickey and the Major Leagues. His Monarchs lost, without compensation from the Major Leagues, Jackie Robinson, Hank Thompson, Ernie Banks, Ellston Howard, Connie Johnson, and Willard Brown among others.[47]

Jackie Robinson took the field as second baseman for the Brooklyn Dodgers on April 15, 1947, before a crowd of 26,623. Satchel was forty. Even though his magical pitching had driven the debate on integration for decades, Major League clubs looked past him because of his age.

Satchel was discouraged but not defeated. He recalled, "I promised myself I'd keep throwing until someone figured they needed me bad in the major leagues." Lahoma stood right at his side, urging him on. Satchel said, "Lahoma made sure I kept thinking that way, too. If I forgot for just a minute, she'd be there reminding me."[48]

No calls came for him from the Major Leagues in 1947. Satchel was forced to watch from the sidelines as Larry Doby, Hank Thompson, Willard Brown, and Dan Bankhead played in the Majors. Others such as Roy Campanella and Don Newcombe were now playing in the Minors.

Winter meetings 1948 and spring training came, but no calls. The 1948 season began. Injuries occurred. Roster moves were made. June arrived but still no calls.

Then the call came. After Satchel got off the phone, he and Lahoma "whooped and hollered and started dancing and [they] didn't stop until [they] danced through every room in the house and were out onto the porch."[49]

Satchel's tryout with the Cleveland Indians was set for July 7, his forty-second birthday. That day the usually cool Satchel Paige was a wreck. Indians' owner Bill Veeck met him at the ballpark to show him the way to the locker room so that he could change into his uniform.

When Satchel walked out onto the field player-manager Lou Boudreau was standing next to Veeck. Boudreau peppered Satchel with questions: "Can you still throw like you used to?" "Can you do that against major leaguers?" Satchel smiled. "Don't you worry about that. The plate's the same size up here."[50]

He began throwing balls to Boudreau. After a while the manager stood up from his squat and told Satchel, "That's some control. You didn't miss the strike zone more'n four times out of fifty. Let's see if you can do that good when I try hitting against you now."[51]

Boudreau was leading the Majors in hitting at .400. Satchel threw to him as long as he wanted. All Boudreau could manage was a single pop fly. The manager flipped his bat toward the dugout and told Veeck, "Don't let him get away. We can use this one."[52]

After Satchel showered and dressed, Veeck came to him with a contract. There was no hesitation. "I signed that contract real quick," Satchel said. He then asked Veeck if he could send some money to J.L.'s Monarchs since they had saved his career when his arm went dead. Without hesitation Veeck cut a check for $5,000 to the Monarchs.[53]

Two days after signing, Satchel was called on to pitch. It was the fifth inning of a night game with his club trailing the Browns 4–1. As he gave Satchel the ball, his manager told him, "Satch, you've got nothing to fear. Don't be scared if they hit you. Pitch loose like you always do."[54]

The first batter singled. That was it. Satchel went to work: single windup—double windup—triple windup—hesitation windup—"step-n-pitch"—side arm—bat dodger.[55] He set them down without a run for two innings. When the Browns' manager saw Satchel's hesitation pitch, he protested to the crew chief. The pitch was ruled legal.

Shortly after Satchel's first game, Will Harbridge, president of the American League, banned his hesitation pitch. After the ruling from on high, Satchel became concerned that if he used any of his other windups "he might ban them too." It was clear to Satchel that Harbridge "didn't want [him] to show up those boys who were young enough to be [his] sons," so he had no choice but to go conservative. He decided to play the "right way" by throwing only his "plain stuff" in the Major Leagues.[56]

On August 3, 1948, Satchel's team was one game behind the Philadelphia A's in the race for the pennant. Satchel was called on to start his first Major League game that night in Cleveland against the Washington Senators. A record crowd of 72,562 filled the stands on a warm midwestern night to see Satchel pitch. Satchel got a quick out to start the game. Then his control abandoned him. He walked the next two batters and yielded a triple to Ed Stewart to hand the Senators a 2–0 lead. After the first inning Satchel put up nothing but zeros. When he left the game in the seventh, his team was up 4–2. They went on to win the game 5–3. With the A's losing, Satchel's team pulled into a tie for first.

Satchel caused a near riot with his next start at Comiskey Park in Chicago. The official game attendance read 51,013, but thousands more crashed through a gate and pushed into the park after a set of turnstiles broke down.[57] It was a tense affair, knotted at 0–0 through four innings. Satchel's team went ahead 1–0 in the top of the fifth, then 2–0 in the eighth, 5–0 in the ninth. When Satchel took the mound in the bottom of the ninth, the Chicago crowd cheered wildly for his every pitch. Facing a first and third threat with only one out, Satchel bore down on the final two batters to finish out his first complete-game Major League shutout.

"Black bastard!" yelled a Washington Senator player at Satchel after being struck out by him that summer. Satchel instinctively made a slight move toward the man. He stopped himself, however, believing it was better to absorb the racial slur than to start a fight.[58]

Satchel's team ended the season in a tie with the Boston Red Sox. After defeating the Red Sox 8–3 in a one-game playoff at Fenway Park, the Indians went on to face the Boston Braves in the World Series—their first appearance in twenty-eight years.

Satchel's chances of pitching in the 1948 World Series were low since the Indians had a strong starting rotation, which often didn't need relief. It included Bob Feller, Bob Lemon, and Gene Beardon. He finally got his chance with a runner on first and one out in the seventh inning of Game Five with the Indians trailing 11–5. Even with the lopsided score against the home team, cheers rocked the stadium as Satchel walked to the mound.

Satchel spit on his fingers and wiped them off on his pants

to get rid of the moisture. The home plate umpire called for the ball so he could inspect it with great suspicion. With the count 1-0 on Warren Spahn, the home plate umpire stopped Satchel mid-motion and came to the mound to explain that he needed to throw in one continuous motion.

After Satchel got Spahn for the second out of the inning, Tommy Holmes strolled to the plate for the Braves. Satchel started his delivery by reaching high and bringing his hands down against his chest—all legal. Again mid-motion another umpire came running. "Balk, balk," he yelled. "You wiggled the fingers of your glove."[59] Satchel was mad but didn't say a thing. He just reared back and threw his "real trouble ball" to the next batter to end the inning.

It wasn't only umpires and league presidents who gave Satchel a hard time. When Satchel went to shake hands with the St. Louis Browns' white catcher, Clint Courtney, the stocky Alabaman just stood there staring at him. Clint flat out refused to catch Satchel. He wouldn't budge an inch. Day after day Satchel kept needling Clint to let him know where he was if he ever wanted a piece of him.

Then one day later that fall, team owner Veeck spotted Satchel and Clint sitting together in the bullpen talking up a storm. Veeck pulled Clint aside to ask him what was up, "Why the change?" "I like the guy," Clint answered. "Just sitting out there talking to him, I've learned more about calling a game than I ever knew in my life."[60]

Toward the end of the season, Veeck was schmoozing his way around town when he ran into Satchel and Clint at a mixed-race nightclub. When Veeck sat down to join them, Clint told him, "My daddy is coming up when we get back to St. Louis. He's going to see me sitting in the bullpen talking to this Paige and he's gonna jump right over the fence and try to give me a whupping." Clint paused to look at Satchel and then told

Veeck, "But Satch and I have it figured out that the two of us can whup him no matter what happens."[61]

Satchel finished the 1948 campaign with six wins against just one loss. That half season he pitched in twenty-one games representing 72.2 innings while posting a 2.48 ERA with forty-three strikeouts. He pitched in the Majors until he was forty-seven years old.

There was nothing Satchel loved as much as playing the Yankees just to drive their manager, Casey Stengel, crazy. In tight games Stengel paced up and down the dugout yelling at his players, "OK now boys, it's the seventh inning and I wants you to get me them hits now. I mean now! Because if you don't get them you know what's going to happen in the ninth? They're going to put in old Father Time and he ain't going to give you nothing."[62] Stengel selected Satchel to play in the 1953 All-Star game. Satchel was enshrined in the Baseball Hall of Fame in 1971.

• • •

Satchel always loved the freedom of driving himself to ball games. At that time driving oneself represented a huge sense of freedom for a black man in a hostile world. He thought nothing of driving across the entire Midwest, often with a stop along the side of the road to camp for the night.

For Satchel there wasn't much better in the whole wide world than just pulling off the road and cooking up a meal. He would pull out his trusty Coleman and get a pan nice and hot with a little fat. Then he cut up some onions real fine and cook them till they were brown. Next he threw in about two pounds of ground chuck—never that super-lean stuff. When that got all brown, he added in a big can of Campbell's Pork & Beans and a number 2 can of Del Monte tomatoes.[63] Satchel had a 1939 Cadillac, the one with the extra wide running boards, the perfect place to sit, like in a pew in a church, while he cooked his meal and enjoyed it real hot.

Stars would come out, and it was like his guitar would just pop right out of its case. There was something special about playing on his Spanish guitar just to the stars and himself. He was just crazy about calypso but not to forget the rhumbas, congas, and boleros. And when it got dark and he was starting to get real tired, that was time for the blues. He would put out his stove and get the blanket from his trunk and just sleep right there. Hell, he thought he slept better than in any fancy bed he had ever slept on. Nothing beat just being out under the stars with his guitar—all by his lonesome self.

20

"El Gamo"

Tetelo was immediately recognizable when he walked onto a baseball field, back straight, chin up, proud, modest with a chiseled jawline, sly smile, and friendly brown eyes. He stood five feet ten and weighed 160 pounds with hardly an ounce of fat. El Gamo (the wild deer) is what many fans called him as a tribute to his extraordinary speed, for El Gamo was one of the fastest men to ever play baseball. At twenty-five he was clocked circling the bases in a head-shaking 13.02 seconds.[1] That same year he raced against Olympic champion Jesse Owens in a one-hundred-meter race and won.[2]

To most fans on the island where he was born, however, he was simply Tetelo. Juan "Tetelo" Vargas was born to a shoe-maker and his wife in the spring of 1906. The Vargas family lived on Calle 19 de Marzo among the crowded streets of Santo Domingo's old colonial district, in the days before the city's name was changed to Ciudad Trujillo. There Tetelo grew up playing sandlot ball with his older brothers, Eduardo "Guagua" and Juan Rafael.[3]

The players for the two capital-city teams, Licey and Escogido, were his childhood idols. When he was just seventeen, Tetelo signed his first professional baseball contract to play for the Escogido Lions, where he joined his older brothers. By the mid-1920s Tetelo was an established star in the Dominican Republic.

By the late 1920s Tetelo had extended his baseball travels to Venezuela, Colombia, and Puerto Rico. In the segregated United States of the 1930s, he became a star as well. Tetelo consistently hit over .300 combined at times with surprising power. While playing with House of David of the Negro American League in 1931, he hit seven straight home runs over a two-game stretch. His speed of course allowed him to accomplish this feat as some of the home runs were of the "inside-the-park" variety.[4]

As teams formed for the 1936 Dominican baseball series, everyone expected Tetelo to sign with Escogido. But Escogido was stubbornly insisting that he play at shortstop, and Tetelo insisted on playing centerfield. To the shock of the capital-city fans, he signed to play with the Estrellas Orientales from the sugar capital down the coast, San Pedro de Macorís.[5] His fans smiled at what they believed to be merely a passing fancy. Yes, they told themselves, Tetelo is a star, but even a star of his caliber could not possibly pull a weak provincial team like the Estrellas into contention for the title. They were positive that the two capital-city teams would dominate as usual. More importantly they believed that after this brief fling with the provincials, Tetelo would come to his senses and return to the capital city.

To the amazement of the Dominican baseball world, Tetelo's outstanding play and leadership drove the Estrellas to their first championship in 1936. In fact the Estrellas so far outstripped their haughty capital rivals that they chose to quit rather than play on, out of sheer dejection once they were mathematically eliminated.

Tetelo for his part so loved playing in San Pedro de Macorís that he moved from Santo Domingo to the smaller city forty-nine miles down the coast. During the 1936 championship run, baseball fever seized the city. Civic leaders raised money and quickly built a five-thousand-seat ballpark during the season and named it Campo Deportivo Tetelo Vargas after their thirty-year-old star.[6] To this day a rebuilt version of Tetelo Vargas Stadium stands as the center of baseball life in that city.

Famously there was the 1937 series in which Tetelo's Estrellas faced the best talent that Rafael Trujillo could buy. Just as Dihigo carried the Santiago team on his shoulders, Tetelo carried the Estrellas, keeping them in the lead of the series until Trujillo filled his Dragones with possibly the greatest assortment of talent ever assembled on one team.

Dominican baseball was not up and running again in a serious way until 1941, when it once again was used as a means to promote a Trujillo election campaign. Trujillo had lain low internationally for nearly two years after the international crisis he had created with the massacre of the Haitians in 1937. Then in late 1939, he opened serious negotiations with the United States to end its control of Dominican customs collections under the 1924 treaty. Once an agreement was reached, Trujillo had himself appointed "ambassador extraordinary on special mission" so that he could travel to Washington DC to personally sign the new treaty granting financial independence to his country for the first time since the 1890s. The news of the treaty signing set off genuinely jubilant demonstrations in the streets of Ciudad Trujillo. Trujillo was voted the new title "restorer of financial independence" by the National Congress on September 26, 1940, probably the only title he was ever granted that had a semblance of merit.[7]

Thus when the 1941 baseball tournament opened on March 29, 1941, the year before the 1942 elections, Trujillo decided to name it "Restauración Financiera" (Financial Restoration [Series]). The series pitted the Estrellas Orientales against Perucho Cepeda's Brujos (Sorcerers), Puerto Rico's championship team. Playing on Cepeda's team was Satchel Paige. Tetelo roamed center field for the Estrellas and hit .448 as the Estrellas took the series from the Brujos.[8]

In 1953 at the age of forty-seven, Tetelo again played baseball in the Dominican Republic. That year he took the league batting title with an average of .355.[9] His final season came in 1955, when he played in six games for his beloved Estrellas and batted .294.[10] Tetelo died of cancer at the age of sixty-five in Guayama, Puerto Rico. He was buried beside his wife, Violeta, in El Cementerio Municipal de Guayama.[11]

Tetelo is enshrined in the Cuban, Dominican, Puerto Rican, and Latin American Halls of Fame. He deserves to be in the American Baseball Hall of Fame.

21

Y Otras

Perhaps the finest group of baseball players ever assembled played in Trujillo's 1937 series. Martín Dihigo, Satchel Paige, Tetelo Vargas, and Josh Gibson were titans. And others like Cool Papa Bell, Perucho Cepeda, Luis Tiant, but for the color of their skin, would today be mentioned in the same breath as Ty Cobb, Honus Wagner, and Carl Hubbell.

James "Cool Papa" Bell arrived in the Dominican Republic in late spring, after his friend Satchel convinced him that the money was too good and the times too high to take a pass. His first game for the Dragones was on May 22, 1937, the twenty-fourth game of the series. At that time the only baseball player in the world who may have been as fast as Cool Papa was playing against him: Tetelo Vargas. Like Tetelo Cool Papa was far from one-dimensional; in addition to running like the wind, he could hit and field. With a sure glove combined with an instinct for the ball, he was able to play a shallow center field, daring batters to hit the ball over his head. During the series Cool Papa batted .318, stretching out fully one-third of his hits into extra bases. Again and again he got on base to be knocked home by Josh Gibson. In the final sixteen games, he scored fourteen runs.

Just like Satchel Cool Papa was banned from the Negro Leagues for jumping to the Dominican Republic, so later that summer when Cool Papa came back to America, he joined Satchel's merry band of Ciudad Trujillo barnstormers. Then for the next four years, he passed up Negro League baseball to play in the Mexican Leagues. Cool Papa's time in Mexico found him at the height of his powers. His finest season was 1940 in Veracruz, when he won the triple crown by batting .437 with 12 home runs and 79 RBIs. With his speed he added 29 doubles, 15 triples, and scored 119 runs—all of this in just eighty-nine games. His team won the championship that year.

In the mid-1940s Cool Papa returned to the Negro Leagues to play for the Pittsburgh Homestead Grays. When at age forty-three he was on the verge of winning the batting title with a .402 average, he learned that young Monte Irvin was being looked at seriously by the white Major Leagues. Cool Papa decided to sit out the final game of the season in order to allow Irvin to win the batting title and improve his prospects of signing with the Major Leagues.[1]

Like so many aging Negro Leaguers, Cool Papa finished his career with the Kansas City Monarchs. When he finally retired from baseball in 1950 at age forty-seven, he had no pension and little savings, so for the next twenty years he was forced to work as a custodian and night security guard at St. Louis City Hall.

Cool Papa was inducted into the American Baseball Hall of Fame in 1974, three years after Satchel. Upon his selection he noted with little bitterness, "At that time the doors were not open only in baseball, but in other avenues that we couldn't enter. They say that I was born too soon. I say the doors were opened too late."[2]

When Cool Papa died in 1991 at age eighty-seven, he requested in his will that his coffin be carried by twelve pallbearers, six black, six white.[3] To honor him St. Louis named the street he lived on Cool Papa Bell Street. Today this street regularly appears in the news as the location of shootings.

Pedro "Perucho" Cepeda was one of the few Puerto Ricans to play in the 1937 series. Today he is primarily remembered as the father of hall of famer Orlando Cepeda, yet many who saw both men thought the father may have been the better player.

When Aybar recruited Perucho for the Dragones, he had seen him shine as a shortstop with a rifle arm and a bad ball hitter capable of hitting for average and power. Perucho had first played in the Dominican Republic as a twenty-four-year-old on the 1929 Sandino team. He next visited the island for a series of exhibition games with Ponce in 1933 and again in 1934 and 1936 as a member of the Escogido team from Ciudad Trujillo.

Perucho likely received the biggest payday up to that point in his career when he signed to play for the 1937 Dragones. Yet it may have been his worst season as a professional player. He made his debut playing first base in the nineteenth game of the series. The Dragones beat the Estrellas 4–1 that day. Perucho had no hits yet made two errors. He played in only five more games. After the arrival of Josh, Cool Papa, and the other Negro Leaguers, Perucho sat on the bench. In six total games he batted .125 and made five errors.

When the 1937 Dominican series ended, Perucho caught a steamer back to Puerto Rico. A mere ten weeks later his son, Orlando, was born. Not long afterward, he joined the Guayama Brujos of the newly formed Puerto Rican Professional Baseball League (commonly known as the Puerto Rican Winter League). As the Brujos' star player, he led the new league in its first two seasons with batting averages of .465 and .383.[4]

The 1939 Puerto Rican season was a virtual reunion of players from Trujillo's 1937 series. Joining Perucho on the Brujos was the familiar battery of Satchel and Cy. Tetelo roamed center field. They often played the Santurce Cangrejeros (Crabbers), who were managed by Josh Gibson. One day when the two teams met, Josh pitched a third of an inning and filled in at first and third bases.[5] That season Satchel led the league in victories with a 19-3 record and struck out 208 batters in 205 innings.[6]

In order to better support his family, Perucho was forced to take a job with the San Juan Water Department in the 1940s. While he continued to play in the Puerto Rican Winter League, baseball became secondary. At age fifty Perucho died of complications from a malarial infection. His son, Orlando, used the five-hundred-dollar signing bonus from his first professional contract to bury his father.[7] Today Perucho is a member of the Puerto Rican Baseball Hall of Fame.

Luis E. Tiant, like Perucho Cepeda, is largely known as the father of a famous son, Luis C. Tiant of Boston Red Sox fame. His contemporaries called him "Sir Skinny" or simply "Lefty."

Fellow Cuban Martín Dihigo recruited Luis to play for the 1937 Águilas. In his first start Luis pitched well but lost to the Dragones 3–1.[8] And on May 2, 1937, he was one of three pitchers to hold the Dragones to two runs in a 3–2 victory.[9]

The following weekend Luis took the mound against Satchel Paige. Luis was chased from the game after allowing two triples, a single, and two runs, without recording an out. That day his team lost 8–5.[10] He rebounded from this disastrous outing the following Sunday with a 6–2 win over the Dragones.[11]

It was downhill from there. Luis lost to the Dragones 12–2 and 6–1 in his two June outings, so at the beginning of July, he headed back home early with other Cuban players.[12] Clearly he had been released.

In October 1937 as a member of the Gavilanes (Hawks), Luis traveled to Venezuela, where he played alongside Tetelo Vargas.[13] Next he appeared on the American baseball scene with the New York Cubans in 1939 and posted a 1-2 record. His first and only child, Luis Clemente, was born the following year in Marianao, Cuba, on November 23, 1940.[14]

It wasn't until 1947, at the age of forty, that the senior Tiant had his best season. He posted a 10-0 record with the New York Cubans, leading his team to the Negro National League pennant and ultimately to victory in the Negro League World Series.

Luis taught his son many of his pitching skills: a tricky delivery, the art of changing speeds, nasty breakings balls, and of course a deadly, deceptive pickoff move. By 1960 young Luis was splitting his time between Cuba and Mexico. Then while Luis was pitching for the Mexico City Tigers in 1961, tensions between the United States and Cuba caused a complete break between the two countries, including a ban on travel.

When the Mexico City Tigers ended their 1961 season, young Luis planned to return home to Cuba. Although it broke his heart, his father urged him not to return and instead to sign a contract with the Cleveland Indians. Heeding his father's advice, the younger Tiant defected to the United States, knowing that he might never see his parents again.[15]

Young Luis began his American career in the Indians' farm system playing for their Charleston, South Carolina, team. There he tasted his first bitter dose of American racism. He recalled, "I couldn't speak very good English but I understand racism. They treated me like a dog, but when I got to Portland, I didn't have any problems."[16]

The years rolled by, and young Luis blossomed into a Major League Baseball star. He won twenty-one games with a 1.60 ERA while pitching four consecutive shutouts in 1968. And between 1973 and 1976, he posted twenty, twenty-two, eighteen, and twenty-one victories for the Boston Red Sox.

During all those years, young Luis and his growing family could not see his parents. The best Luis Sr., who now earned his living by pumping gas, could do was to watch his son pitch on national games of the week that he was able to view by pointing large antennae toward Florida to pick up local television stations.[17] Ironically it was failed presidential candidate and South Dakota Senator George McGovern who took up Tiant's issue up with Cuban dictator Fidel Castro in May 1975.[18] Three months after McGovern's charm offensive, Luis's parents were allowed to fly to Boston for a joyful reunion with their son and his family.[19] Luis Sr. and his wife Isabel stayed in the United States into the fall and were able to watch their son pitch the Boston Red Sox to a 6–0 victory in the first game of the 1975 World Series.

When the seventy-year-old father, wearing a brown suit and a brown hat, visited the Boston clubhouse after the game, he had only one comment for reporters: "He's better than me."[20]

A little more than a year after his parents saw their son pitch in the World Series, they died within three days of each other. They were buried side by side in the cemetery at Milton, Massachusetts.[21] "My father," Luis insisted, "was a better pitcher than me."[22]

Luis E. Tiant Sr. was elected to the Cuban Baseball Halls of Fame in 1964. His son joined him there in 1997.

To understand the level of talent in the 1937 series, it is worth mentioning the other players today in halls of fame: Alejandro Oms (Cuban Baseball Hall of Fame), Santos Amaro (Mexican Baseball Hall of Fame), Lazaro Salazar (Cuban and Venezuelan Baseball Halls of Fame), and Horatio Martínez (Latino Baseball Hall of Fame).

Epilogue

Tenth Inning

This is not really a story about baseball. It's a story about power. A dictator on a Caribbean Island decided he needed to rent the best baseball players to win a series dedicated to his "reelection." This dictator turned to perhaps the most talented baseball players who every played the game—black American players who were so powerless in their own country that they were relegated to playing for little money, on shabby fields before small, mainly poor, mostly black crowds.

Oddly this confluence of events brought to the small island the best championship series ever played. Despite the small stage on which the "Championship Dedicated to the Reelection of Rafael Trujillo" played, it had every element of a great series. World class talent, extreme drama, skullduggery, high stakes and lots of money. But few outside the small island knew the series had even happened.

When Satchel and his trusted friend and catcher boarded a charter plane and arrived in Ciudad Trujillo, they experienced a great paradox: they were in a dictatorship where all things ran at the whim of one man, but they quickly realized that they were no longer living under the oppressive weight of segregation. While this tropical island might not have had freedom of the press or habeas corpus, without Jim Crow pulling them down, Satchel and his friends had the freedom to enjoy restaurants, hotels, stores, country clubs, golf courses, beaches, bars, and brothels-places they could never set foot on in "the land of the free and the home of the brave."

It's been over a hundred years since Satchel Paige was born into the poverty of a segregated Southern city. And it's been over forty years since he pitched his last game. Satchel played for most of his career in the obscurity of the Negro Leagues simply because he was barred by his race from playing on the grand stage of the major leagues until he was nearly two decades past his prime. Moreover, he lived in the days before television cameras could beam his image into millions of homes. Yet his name still rings loudly through the fog of time. And as the names of his then famous contemporaries fade from our collective memories, Satchel's only grows. It grows because he was one of those unforgettable personalities who sounded a resonant chord with his generation. And that sound has carried to the generations beyond his time. Satchel Paige is a name that deserves to be mentioned in the same breath as Muhammad Ali or Babe Ruth.

No more talented or colorful figure ever played the game of baseball than Satchel Paige. It is hard to believe that he pitched year around, with only one break for an arm injury, for over 30 years between 1926 and 1957. Yet it is estimated that he pitched in more than 2,500 games with over 100 no-hitters. Satchel would start his yearly rounds in the Caribbean, Mexico or South America—playing in leagues as far flung as Venezuela, Cuba, Mexico and Puerto Rico. By spring he was back in America, speeding from town to town in his latest roadster—oftentimes stopping by the roadside to cook his dinner over a camp stove and entertain himself by strumming his guitar until he fell asleep under the stars on the floorboard of his car. If he was playing in the Negro leagues he would earn extra money by squeezing in exhibition games between scheduled league starts. To fill out the year he would often drive to California and spend the fall months pitching in a combination of fall league and exhibition games against white major leaguers.

What is most remarkable about Satchel Paige is his perseverance. Perseverance in the face of a society that only allowed him to play in the major leagues when he was well past his prime. Perseverance in the face of rules which were changed on the fly to disadvantage him simply because he would have made their best hitters look bad at the plate. And more than anything, perseverance in the face of a society which used it power to degrade, humiliate and strip of liberty all members of his race.

APPENDIX

Notes on Paige's Magical Pitching

The progress of that ball is historic, for it travels as no ball,
not even Dizzy Dean's or Dazzy Vance's or Walter Johnson's,
ever traveled. It is like lightning striking out of a sleepy
summer-day cloud. It strikes and it is a strike.

—LLOYD LEWIS's description of Satchel Paige's fastball

In 1934 Satchel spent a warm winter in Los Angeles singing on
the radio and hurling baseballs for the Royal Colored Giants—a
team the *Los Angeles Times* called a "dusky squad."[1] Before throwing his last game of the winter season in Los Angeles, he headed
120 miles south down the California coast to San Diego to pitch
and sing at a benefit game for the widow of the black manager
of the Mission Stars, Henry "Pete" Grant.

The *San Diego Sun* headlined their preview piece "PAIGE TO
CROON BEFORE BENEFIT" and wrote, "Paige, one of the greatest of colored pitchers and also a crooner of Los Angeles radio
fame, will offer several ballads over the public address system
before he takes the mound."[2] How Satchel must have loved getting higher billing for his singing than his pitching.

It was a cloudy February Friday in San Diego, California. Even
though it was the height of the Great Depression, it was a day
to relax, Washington's Birthday, 1935. In the stands that day at
Balboa Park's City Stadium sat sixteen-year-old Ted Williams,
who had scraped together his pennies to watch Satchel Paige
pitch.[3] He could hardly get over the sight of Satchel when he

took the mound—Williams saw a pitcher so skinny he had trouble holding his pants up.[4] Satchel delivered an overpowering performance that day, striking out seventeen batters while giving up just two hits. The *San Diego Sun* wrote, "[Paige] doesn't need anything but a catcher when he's on the mound."[5] The *San Diego Union* enthused, "The elongated colored twirler exhibited blinding speed and miraculous control."[6]

This single game made an indelible impression on young Ted Williams. Decades later, when Williams sat down to write *The Science of Hitting*, he referenced this game: "I saw him first when I was a kid player in San Diego. There's no question he was one of the greatest, especially then. I hit against him [years later] four or five times and I kept saying to myself, 'Boy, what a pitcher this guy must have been.' I was impressed with his delivery, his easy, deceptive motion. All the time he was moving around on the mound, throwing from different angles, different windups. He'd stretch with the bases empty just to throw you off. He got me out every time that day."[7]

It's a shame that because he played mostly in the days before television and instant replay, very little was written about Satchel Paige's pitching. Many of his techniques run contrary to the received wisdom of our day, which stresses repetitive motion and creates a predictability, which Satchel would have found intolerable.

After praising Paige Ted Williams lays out a simple proposition: "Pitchers should be told: Move around the mound, try a little side arm, change the tempo. Anything to upset that picture over the shoulder. Upset that and you upset the batter. If you've got two pitches and one delivery, you've got two pitches, period. Two pitches and two deliveries, that's four pitches."[8]

As Ted Williams knew, simple math tells the story. Assume that the average Major League pitcher has three pitches, a predictable delivery, throws off the same spot on the rubber, and has one arm slot. The odds of guessing what is coming at you are 1 in 3. After 1939 Paige had nine pitches, three-plus wind-ups, four general locations off the rubber, plus three arm slots. A batter would have the odds of 1 in 324 at guessing Satchel's pitch correctly. And that's not even factoring in any variation in the location of the pitch. Satchel Paige understood Ted Williams's powerful equation better than anyone.

Satchel began his career as a speedball pitcher with preternatural control. From the beginning he had mastered the art of bending his fastball. The report from his first professional game talks of the "airtight pitching of a long, lanky black boy by the name of Satchell" and refers to his pitches as "mysterious curves."[9] One umpire who saw him pitch in the 1940s said his fastball "sounded as if a swarm of killer bees was coming down the pike, humming all the way."[10] Many others simply described it as an aspirin tablet.[11] When Dominican fans gathered to watch Satchel at his first practice on the island, they were amazed at the sound his fastballs made as they popped in the catcher's mitt. *Bolas relámpagos* (lightening balls), they kept saying as they shook their heads in disbelief.[12]

It was as a teenager at an Alabama "reform" school that Satchel learned to kick up his foot to make it appear like "it was blacking out the sky" and to "swoop" his arm around and release the ball when it "was right in the batter's face."[13] Today's best pitching coaches teach both of these techniques. The high leg kick adds velocity to a fastball, while the late release point gives a pitcher two important advantages: First, it obscures the release point of the ball. Second, it subtracts a few extra feet from the distance the ball has to travel, thereby cutting down the hitter's time to react.[14]

As a teenager Satchel also picked up his habit of studying a batter's knees for signs of weakness. In the 1952 season switch hitter Mickey Mantle hit a left-handed home run off Satchel in his first at bat. Mantle then changed over and batted right handed for the rest of the game, which prompted Satchel to keep asking his teammates, "Where is the boy that done me the injury?"[15]

So how was Satchel able to pitch so well for so long? Largely on his own, he developed a unique style of pitching that allowed him to throw unheard of numbers of innings and created such a great degree of variation from one pitch to the next that it was nearly impossible for an opposing batter to get comfortable in the batter's box or to time a pitch. As Ted Williams testified: "Satchel Paige had about fifteen different deliveries. He was always changing that tempo. I am sure much of the reason for Satchel Paige's fantastic longevity was that he threw the ball so many different ways. He had motion, he had control. He went through a stuff period when nobody had more stuff. He went through a period where he was coy, and hesitating and could just mesmerize you. You'd watch all that and whoom, he'd blow it past you."[16]

After six-feet-five, 220-pound Tiger first baseman Walt "Moose" Dropo swung wildly at two of Satchel's deceptive offerings during the 1952 season, he "lost his head and accused him of showboating." Satchel replied with his best fastball. Dropo spun himself into the ground with the seat of his pants facing the stands. "My, my, talk about showboatin'," Satchel remarked.[17]

Paige's Pitches

Before the fall of 1938, Satchel relied on variations of his fastball, all thrown with pinpoint precision from three different arm slots, with special windups, all from various spots on the pitching rubber. He also had a way of changing speeds on his fast ball, calling the slower one "little tom" and his really fast flavor "long tom."[18]

We have been left the best descriptions of his famous fastball by those like Quincy Trouppe who saw him in his prime: "That day I learned why Satchel's fast ball was so deceptive. He had long, wiry arms. His stride was long also, and with his long, strong fingers he could put such tremendous back spin on his fast ball that it would rise two to four inches while traveling from his hand to the batter. This is why his fast ball looked like a marble to the batter, and I think most players who hit against Satch would agree."[19]

Jump Ball—Satchel threw his "jump ball" by placing his fingers across the seams, making his fastball "jump four to six inches."[20]

Be Ball or Bee-Line Ball—Satchel's explanation for his "be ball" was very simple: "My be ball is a be ball 'cause it 'be' right where I want it." He threw this fastball with his fingers "on the smooth hide."[21]

Following the arm injury that sidelined Satchel for a year, he regained his place on the pitcher's mound in 1939 against daunting odds. But inevitably his fastball went from one of the fastest in history to a better than average one—he went from blinding speed to blazing speed, which he had to save for spots. So for the next few years he developed an amazing arsenal of pitches to go with his occasional fastball.

The "Stuff" Period

Ted Williams remembered "nobody had more stuff" than Satchel. When fellow Mobile, Alabamian, Willie Mays met Satchel in the late 1940s, he was stunned at his repertoire of windups, releases, and pitches. Mays said,

> He showed me the darnedest stuff I ever saw, along with some of the screwiest motions and combinations of different speeds. Old Satchel could really drive you crazy. He had a knuckleball, a screwball, an assortment of curves—and his hesitation pitch. He'd pump his arm around like a windmill, and bring it over his head, and you expected to see the ball coming down, because that's the point at which a pitcher would throw. But nothing happened. He would be almost in his follow-through when all of the sudden the darn ball would appear and you would be swinging way in front of it.[22]

The most striking thing about Satchel's transformation is that he always kept his pinpoint control, even when throwing the most outrageous "stuff" from the most unorthodox wind-ups and angles.

Curve—For purposes of comparison, it is safe to say that Satchel never had a traditional curveball. He developed a slow curve as more of an off-speed pitch. He explained, "My curve is never fast. I never break it off. Might crack a bone in my wrist. Just a slow curve to fool 'em. The batters can't believe it from me. They hear about my speed and they can't believe the curve when they see it. I use it for strike three when I have him three and two. I got seventeen strikeouts in one day this summer on men waiting in that three-and-two spot for a fast one and then gettin' a slow curve."[23]

Whipsy-dipsy-do—Satchel's "whipsy-dipsy-do" may be a unique pitch in the annals of baseball. It was a forkball that he threw either sidearm or submarine—he said it that "slithers or slinks." He threw it thumb off the ball with "three fingers. The middle finger sticks up high, like a bent fork."[24]

Blooper—What Satchel called his "blooper" was probably reminiscent of "Rip" Sewell's famous Eephus pitch.[25]

Two-Hump Blooper—This was a special change-up with extra movement.[26]

The Barber—The "barber" was a submarine pitch that started low and ended up riding high and tight to the batter.[27]

Bat Dodger—Satchel even developed a knuckleball that he named his "bat dodger."

Nothing Ball—Nothing more than Satchel's clever name for his change-up.

Walking the Rubber

Satchel was constantly changing the angle of pitches by varying the part of the rubber he touched with his foot for each pitch—yet he consistently threw strikes. He called it "walking the rubber," insisting that he would never "pitch from the same spot twice." Instead he would feel out the right angle for each batter. He described it as "somethin' like radar."[28]

Three Deliveries

Consider this: It has been estimated that during Satchel Paige's career he pitched 2,500 games. Some years he pitched 150 games. He pitched as a professional from 1926 to 1961. He is the only pitcher in Major League history who was able to pitch effectively into his fifties. How was this possible?

Both Satchel and Ted Williams had a simple explanation: Because he threw from three different arm slots overhand, side arm, and submarine, Satchel was able to spread the strain of pitching around to different groups of muscles. As he explained, "I use three sets of these here little biceps. Overhand uses one, way out sideways uses another, and up from down there still another one. That's another reason my arm never does get tired."[29]

Ted Williams also attributed Paige's durability to his different deliveries: "I am sure much of the reason for Satchel Paige's fantastic longevity was that he threw the ball so many different ways."[30]

Windups That Created Chaos

It was probably because he was a musician that Satchel understood tempo—and therefore the importance of disrupting tempo. He had taken up singing and drums as a teen in "reform" school. As he traveled around the South in the mid-1920s, he played with many of the great musicians of his era, sitting in with Louis Armstrong and his band and Jelly Roll Morton.[31] As he was singing and strumming his guitar, Satchel was busy perfecting windups to disrupt the tempo of opposing hitters. He developed his famous hesitation windup as a child perfecting the art of bonking other kids with rocks. He reasoned, "If a man was throwin' at you, you wouldn't just stand there, you'd duck. But if a man started to throw, and you ducked and then he stopped, where would you be? Why you'd be standin' there duckin' with your bare face, ready to be bongoed big as you please. That's exactly how I studied out my hesitation pitch. I start my throw. The target ducks, I hesitate. He's still duckin'. Wham, I got my man. Years later, after some of my pitchin' speed wore out I remembered that old fooler hesitation pitch."[32] While playing for the House of David in 1934, Satchel kept admiring the fulsome beards of his teammates while loudly complaining that he could never grow one. His teammates presented him with a lengthy red beard to wear when he pitched that day. During the elaborate progression of hesitation windup, the beard got caught on his sleeve and was torn from his face during the delivery.[33]

There's no telling exactly how many windups Satchel had in his bag of tricks. At the very least he had a single windup, double windup, triple windup, hesitation windup, no windup, windmill wheel, and "step-n-pitch."[34]

When it became clear to the powers of Major League baseball that Paige's hesitation windup was embarrassing their league's hitters—even though it was legal by the rules—they banned it. To Satchel this ruling didn't make much sense. As he saw it, "Accordin' to the rules a balk is a pitch that fools a base runner. If I take a windup I can't throw to a base. That's the rules. So if I take a hesitation windup, the runner knows I can't throw to pick him off. I ain't foolin' him. I'm foolin' the batter."[35]

Training and Game Preparation

Satchel Paige was ahead of his times in understanding the importance of keeping his stomach and back muscles strong. He knew keeping these muscles strong was what gave him "balance" and reduced the strain on his arm.[36] So while Satchel looked skinny, he was powerful. When Quincy Trouppe caught for Satchel in a North Dakota league in 1934, they had playful wrestling matches. Quincy was astonished at Satchel's strength, and he was "happy to let him go!" Quincy recalled, "I was six-foot-three and weighed fifteen pounds more than Satchel, but he was mighty powerful."[37]

Satchel was adamant about never pitching until he was completely warmed up. He would keep moving from the moment he stepped on the field. "Before the game, I start fielding bunts, then I hit to the infield, then I chase flies, or work out at third, but I never do throw till ever' muscle, ever' single one, is all loosed up," he explained.[38] He would not even sit until he was done pitching the first inning.

Perhaps the most idiosyncratic part of his daily regime was taking a near-scalding bath in the morning, then another one in the evening "so hot nobody else could stand it." He insisted these hot baths kept his arm from "ever gettin' sore," insisting, "It's kept my arm alive."[39]

NOTES

Preface

1. Turkin, *Official Encyclopedia of Baseball*, 506.

1. Trujillo City

1. Newman, "Land Columbus Loved," 208.
2. Newman, "Land Columbus Loved," 208 and plate VII.
3. Gunther, *Inside Latin America*, 440.
4. Walker, *Journey toward the Sunlight*, 80.

2. Time to Get a Job

1. Paige, *Maybe I'll Pitch Forever*, 16–17.
2. Paige, *Pitchin' Man*, 27.
3. Paige, *Maybe I'll Pitch Forever*, 17; Paige, *Pitchin' Man*, 27.
4. Paige, *Maybe I'll Pitch Forever*, 17.
5. Paige, *Maybe I'll Pitch Forever*, 17.
6. The complete date is July 7, 1906. Yet for years Paige deliberately created doubt about his birthdate. In his 1948 account of his life, *Pitchin' Man* (17), he says that his ex-wife Janet saw the date July 28, 1905, written in his mother's Bible. However, a document issued by the Mobile, Alabama, County Health Department in 1954 shows his birthdate as July 7, 1906. The original source for this document is unclear.
7. Thomason, *Mobile*, 169.
8. Paige calls Mount Meigs the Industrial School for Negro Children, which was the name in 1961, when he wrote about it in his book *Maybe I'll Pitch Forever*.
9. Paige, *Pitchin' Man*, 90.
10. Roorda, *Dictator Next Door*, 121.
11. Paige, "My Biggest Baseball Day," 9.
12. Ornes, *Trujillo*, 167.
13. Paige, *Maybe I'll Pitch Forever*, 123–24.
14. Paige, *Maybe I'll Pitch Forever*, 120.
15. Paige, *Pitchin' Man*, 59.

3. Show Me the Money

1. *Chicago Defender*, April 24, 1937.
2. *Chicago Defender*, April 24, 1937.
3. *Chicago Defender*, April 24, 1937.
4. *Chicago Defender*, April 24, 1937.
5. *New Orleans Times Picayune*, March 15, 1937.
6. *New Orleans Times Picayune*, March 17, 1937.
7. *New Orleans Times Picayune*, March 19, 1937.
8. Paige, *Maybe I'll Pitch Forever*, 116.
9. Paige, *Maybe I'll Pitch Forever*, 116–17.
10. Fox, *Satchel Paige's America*, 104–5.
11. Fox, *Satchel Paige's America*, 104–5.
12. Fox, *Satchel Paige's America*, 104–5.
13. T. J. Jones, *Negro Education*, 1917.
14. Hart, *Social Progress of Alabama*.
15. Paige, *Maybe I'll Pitch Forever*, 25.
16. Paige, *Maybe I'll Pitch Forever*, 24.
17. Fox, *Satchel Paige's America*, 85.
18. Fox, *Satchel Paige's America*, 85.
19. Paige, *Maybe I'll Pitch Forever*, 26.
20. Paige, *Maybe I'll Pitch Forever*, 29.

4. Chapita

1. *Listín Diario*, March 5, 1937. Unless otherwise noted, all translations from the Spanish are my own.
2. Ariza, *Trujillo*, 23.
3. Crassweller, *Trujillo*, 26–27.
4. Crassweller, *Trujillo*, 25–26.
5. Moya Pons, *Dominican Republic*, 261.
6. Crassweller, *Trujillo*, 30.
7. Crassweller, *Trujillo*, 31.
8. Welles, *Naboth's Vineyard*, 2:676–78.
9. Crassweller, *Trujillo*, 34.

5. The Americans

1. These wedding vows roughly follow those we are used to: "Do you take as your wife Aminta Ledesma Lachapelle, promising to be faithful, both in prosperity and in adversity, in health as in sickness, loving and respecting her throughout your life?"
2. Crassweller, *Trujillo*, 36–37.
3. Crassweller, *Trujillo*, 35–36.

4. Knight, *Americans in Santo Domingo*, 26–52.
5. Knight, *Americans in Santo Domingo*, 68.
6. Knight, *Americans in Santo Domingo*, 71.
7. Knight, *Americans in Santo Domingo*, 86–90.
8. Espaillat, *Trujillo*, 24.
9. Vega y Pagan, *Military Biography*, 47.
10. Vega y Pagan, *Military Biography*, 55.
11. Hicks, *Blood in the Streets*, 29.
12. Vega y Pagan, *Military Biography*, 160.
13. Crassweller, *Trujillo*, 47.
14. Vega y Pagan, *Military Biography*, 61.
15. Vega y Pagan, *Military Biography*, various.
16. Crassweller, *Trujillo*, 49–50.
17. Roorda, *Dictator Next Door*, 163.
18. Beezley, *Latin American Popular Culture*, 233.
19. Galíndez, *Era of Trujillo*, 10.
20. *La Revista* 2, no. 16 (August 1927).
21. Crassweller, *Trujillo*, 51, Law no. 928.

6. A Long, Lanky Black Boy

1. Paige, *Pitchin' Man*, 24.
2. Paige, *Maybe I'll Pitch Forever*, 36.
3. Donovan, "Fabulous Satchel Paige," 68.
4. Donovan, "Fabulous Satchel Paige," 68.
5. *Chattanooga Times*, May 1, 1926.
6. *Chattanooga Times*, May 2, 1926.
7. *Chattanooga Times*, May 2, 1926.
8. *Chattanooga Times*, July 3, 1926.
9. *Chattanooga Times*, May 6, 1926.
10. *Chattanooga Times*, May 10, 1926. It is possible that the writer may have seen Waddell pitch, for he had played for the Louisville Colonels in 1897 and 1899.
11. Paige, *Maybe I'll Pitch Forever*, 41.
12. Veeck, *Veeck as in Wreck*, 182–83.
13. Paige, *Maybe I'll Pitch Forever*, 42.
14. *Chattanooga Times*, June 12, 1926.
15. Paige, *Maybe I'll Pitch Forever*, 43.
16. Paige, *Maybe I'll Pitch Forever*, 47.
17. Paige, *Maybe I'll Pitch Forever*, 44–45.

7. Trujillo Es El Jefe

1. Crassweller, *Trujillo*, 64.

2. Ornes, *Trujillo*, 56.

3. Hicks, *Blood in the Streets*, 14.

4. Ornes, *Trujillo*, 58.

5. Crassweller, *Trujillo*, 70.

6. Ornes, *Trujillo*, 56.

7. Ornes, *Trujillo*, 58.

8. Galíndez, *Era of Trujillo*, 17.

9. Galíndez, *Era of Trujillo*, 19.

10. Hicks, *Blood in the Streets*, 10.

11. Crassweller, *Trujillo*, 87.

12. Schoenrich, *Santo Domingo*, 71.

13. Ariza, *Trujillo*, 180–81.

14. Ariza, *Trujillo*, 89–90.

15. Besault, *President Trujillo*, 27. Besault worked for Hearst newspapers, and his book provides useful information about the Trujillo era. It is worth keeping in mind, however, that he was paid by Trujillo's administration to write the book.

16. Ornes, *Trujillo*, 63.

17. Hicks, *Blood in the Streets*, 43.

8. Opening Day Away

1. Moya Pons, *Dominican Republic*, 325.

2. *Listín Diario*, March 6, 1937.

3. Inoa and Cruz, *Baseball in Dominican Republic*, 110. Nina was a respected lawyer who had played baseball in the capital city and was appointed judge in San Pedro de Macorís.

4. Inoa and Cruz, *Baseball in Dominican Republic*, 111. Oriente Park, renamed Sports Field Tetelo Vargas on May 1, 1936, "in a supreme desire to recognize the physical and moral virtues of Juan Esteban Vargas," had been built just a year earlier for $2,905 dollars and could hold five thousand fans.

5. *Listín Diario*, March 29, 1937.

6. González Echevarria, *Pride of Havana*, 262–63.

7. *Listín Diario*, March 29, 1937.

8. *Listín Diario*, March 29, 1937.

9. *Listín Diario*, March 29, 1937.

9. Royal Prerogative

1. Inoa and Cruz, *Baseball in Dominican Republic*, 81–82.

2. Inoa and Cruz, *Baseball in Dominican Republic*, 82.

3. Inoa and Cruz, *Baseball in Dominican Republic*, 111.

4. Galíndez, *Era of Trujillo*, 29.

5. This is a curious story itself: Trujillo discovered that President Roosevelt was a stamp collector.

6. Crassweller, *Trujillo*, 50–51.

7. Roorda, *Dictator Next Door*, 103.

8. Crassweller, *Trujillo*, 51.

9. Hicks, *Blood in the Streets*, 65.

10. Crassweller, *Trujillo*, 51.

11. *Listín Diario*, June 5, 1934.

12. *Listín Diario*, December 5, 1934.

13. Galíndez, *Era of Trujillo*, 32.

14. Ornes, *Trujillo*, 214.

15. Galíndez, *Era of Trujillo*, 10.

16. Crassweller, *Trujillo*, 131–32.

17. *Papers relating to the Foreign Relations*, 562.

18. Galíndez, *Era of Trujillo*, 35.

19. *La Opinion*, April 3, 1937.

20. *Listín Diario*, April 4, 1937.

21. *La Opinion*, April 5, 1937.

10. Total Catastrophe

1. Holway, *Voices*, 159.

2. Ingham and Feldman, *African-American Business Leaders*, 299.

3. Ingham and Feldman, *African-American Business Leaders*, 297.

4. Paige, *Maybe I'll Pitch Forever*, 70.

5. Ribowsky, *Don't Look Back*, 260.

6. Cum Posey (Homestead Grays) and Ed Bolden (Philadelphia Stars) were the only owners not tied to the numbers racket. Abe Manley (Newark Eagles), Alex Pompez (New York Cubans), Ed "Soldier Boy" Semler (New York Black Yankees), and Tom Wilson (Baltimore Elite Giants) all made their money in numbers.

7. *Philadelphia Inquirer*, August 18, 1936.

8. *Philadelphia Inquirer*, August 18, 1936.

9. *New York Times*, January 15, 1937.

10. *New York Times*, March 29, 1937.

11. Peterson, *Only the Ball Was White*, 136.

12. *Chicago Defender*, January 16, 1937.

13. *Pittsburgh Courier*, March 6, 1937.

14. *Chicago Defender*, May 1, 1937.

15. *Chicago Defender*, May 1, 1937; and *Pittsburgh Courier*, May 1, 1937.

16. *Pittsburgh Courier*, May 1, 1937.

17. *Pittsburgh Courier*, May 1, 1937.

18. *Pittsburgh Courier*, May 1, 1937.

19. *Pittsburgh Courier*, May 1 and 15, 1937.

20. *Pittsburgh Courier*, May 15, 1937.

21. *Pittsburgh Courier*, May 15, 1937.

22. Fox, *Satchel Paige's America*, 107.

23. *Chicago Defender*, May 29, 1937.

24. Fox, *Satchel Paige's America*, 104.

25. Paige, "My Biggest Baseball Day, 8.

11. The Stars Arrive

1. Besault, *President Trujillo*, 370.

2. Galíndez, *Era of Trujillo*, 33.

3. *Listín Diario*, October 26, 1936.

4. *Listín Diario*, March 30, 1937.

5. *Listín Diario*, April 10, 1937.

6. Inoa and Cruz, *Baseball in Dominican Republic*, 80.

7. Inoa and Cruz, *Baseball in Dominican Republic*, 82.

8. Welles, *Naboth's Vineyard*, 1:34–36.

9. *Listín Diario*, January 29, 2011.

10. Inoa and Cruz, *Baseball in Dominican Republic*, 117.

11. *Listín Diario*, April 12, 1937.

12. *Listín Diario*, April 10, 1937.

13. *Listín Diario*, April 19, 1937.

14. *Listín Diario*, April 19, 1937.

15. González Echevarriía, *Pride of Havana*, 274.

16. *Listín Diario*, April 24, 1937.

17. *Listín Diario*, April 22, 1937.

18. *Listín Diario*, April 22, 1937.

12. Después de la Victoria

1. *Listín Diario*, April 22, 1937.

2. *Listín Diario*, April 21, 1937.

3. *Listín Diario*, April 26, 1937.

4. *Listín Diario*, April 26, 1937.

5. *Listín Diario*, April 28, 1937.

6. *Listín Diario*, April 28, 1937.

7. *Listín Diario*, April 28, 1937.

8. *Listín Diario*, April 30, 1937.

9. *Listín Diario*, April 30, 1937.

10. *Listín Diario*, May 1, 1937.

11. *Listín Diario*, May 3, 1937.

12. *Listín Diario*, May 3, 1937.

13. *Listín Diario*, May 3, 1937.

14. *Listín Diario*, May 3, 1937.

15. *Listín Diario*, May 3, 1937.
16. Fox, *Satchel Paige's America*, 105.

13. Nuevos Rumbos

1. *Listín Diario*, May 31, 1930.
2. Ornes, *Trujillo*, 189–91.
3. *Listín Diario*, May 8, 1937.
4. *Listín Diario*, May 8, 1937.
5. *Listín Diario*, May 8, 1937.
6. *Listín Diario*, May 8, 1937.
7. Hicks, *Blood in the Streets*, 67.
8. *Listín Diario*, May 10, 1930.
9. *Listín Diario*, May 10, 1930.
10. *Listín Diario*, May 14, 1937.
11. *Listín Diario*, May 17, 1937.
12. *Listín Diario*, May 20, 1937.
13. *Listín Diario*, May 22, 1937.
14. *Listín Diario*, May 22, 1937.
15. *Listín Diario*, May 22, 1937.
16. *Listín Diario*, May 24, 1937.
17. *Listín Diario*, May 24, 1937.
18. Paige, "My Biggest Baseball Day," 8.
19. Paige, "My Biggest Baseball Day," 8.
20. Paige, "My Biggest Baseball Day," 8.
21. Paige, *Pitchin' Man*, 58.
22. Paige, "My Biggest Baseball Day," 8.

14. Black Babe Ruth

1. *Chicago Daily Tribune*, June 17, 1937.
2. *Listín Diario*, May 26, 1937.
3. Brashler, *Josh Gibson*, 79.
4. Brashler, *Josh Gibson*, 107.
5. *Listín Diario*, June 11, 1937.
6. *Listín Diario*, June 12, 1937.
7. *Listín Diario*, June 26, 1937.
8. *Listín Diario*, June 14, 1937.
9. *Listín Diario*, June 21, 1937.
10. *Listín Diario*, June 22, 1937.
11. *Listín Diario*, June 9, 1937.
12. *Listín Diario*, June 11, 1937.
13. *Listín Diario*, June 22, 1937.

14. *Listín Diario*, June 26, 1937.

15. Holway, *Voices*, 112.

15. Fiesta de la Chapita

1. *Listín Diario*, April 28, 1937.

2. Ribowsky, *Power and the Darkness*, 174.

3. *Listín Diario*, June 26, 1937.

4. *Listín Diario*, June 28, 1937.

5. *Listín Diario*, June 28, 1937.

6. *Listín Diario*, June 28, 1937.

7. *Listín Diario*, June 26, 1937.

8. *Listín Diario*, July 1, 1937.

9. *Listín Diario*, July 5, 1937.

10. *Listín Diario*, July 5, 1937.

11. *Listín Diario*, July 5, 1937.

12. *Listín Diario*, July 10, 1937.

13. *Listín Diario*, July 10, 1937.

14. *Listín Diario*, July 10, 1937.

15. *Listín Diario*, July 10, 1937.

16. Holway, *Black Diamonds*, 32.

17. Paige, *Maybe I'll Pitch Forever*, 120.

18. *Listín Diario*, July 12, 1937.

19. Paige, *Pitchin' Man*, 59

20. *Listín Diario*, July 7, 1937.

21. *Listín Diario*, July 7, 1937.

22. *Listín Diario*, July 7, 1937.

23. *Listín Diario*, July 7, 1937.

24. *Afro-American*, July 24, 1937.

25. Riley, *Biographical Encyclopedia*, 403.

26. Paige, *Maybe I'll Pitch Forever*, 119; *Afro-American*, July 24, 1937.

27. *Afro-American*, July 24, 1937.

28. *Listín Diario*, July 13, 1937.

16. The Maestro's Coda

1. *Dallas Morning News*, September 4, 1999.

2. Santana Alonso, *El Inmortal de béisbol*, 78–82.

3. Santana Alonso, *El Inmortal de béisbol*, 78–82.

4. Santana Alonso, *El Inmortal de béisbol*, 119.

5. Santana Alonso, *El Inmortal de béisbol*, 127–28.

6. Santana Alonso, *El Inmortal de béisbol*, 130.

7. *Miami Herald*, May 23, 1971.

8. *Granma* (La Habana), May 31, 1971.

17. The Heartbreaking End of Josh Gibson

1. *Afro-American*, July 31, 1937; *Chicago Defender*, July 31, 1937; and *Pittsburgh Courier*, July 31, 1937.

2. *Pittsburgh Courier*, July 31, 1937

3. *Afro-American*, August 7, 1937.

4. *Washington Post*, April 7, 1939.

5. Holway, *Josh and Satch*, 122–23.

6. Holway, *Josh and Satch*, 163.

7. Brashler, *Josh Gibson*, 130.

8. Ribowsky, *Power and the Darkness*, 271.

9. Holway, *Josh and Satch*, 165.

10. Lawrence D. Hogan. *Shades of Glory: The Negro Leagues and the Story of African-American Baseball*. Washington DC: National Geographic Society, 2006.

11. Brashler, *Josh Gibson*, 128.

12. *Pittsburgh Courier*, March 23, 1946.

13. *Pittsburgh Courier*, May 11, 1946.

14. *Pittsburgh Courier*, May 25, 1946.

15. Ribowsky, *Power and the Darkness*, 294.

16. Holway, *Josh and Satch*, 190.

17. *New York Times*, January 21, 1947.

18. *Pittsburgh Courier*, January 25, 1947.

19. Brashler, *Josh Gibson*, 192–93.

18. The Fall of Trujillo

1. Crassweller, *Trujillo*, 134.

2. Roorda, *Dictator Next Door*, 163.

3. Espaillat, *Trujillo*, 28.

4. Reynolds, "Murder in the Tropics," 34.

5. Crassweller, *Trujillo*, 154.

6. Crassweller, *Trujillo*, 154.

7. Hicks, *Blood in the Streets*, 108.

8. Crassweller, *Trujillo*, 154.

9. Crassweller, *Trujillo*, 156.

10. *New York Times*, October 21, 1937.

11. *New York Times*, October 25, 1937.

12. *Listín Diario*, November 9, 1937.

13. *New York Times*, November 10, 1937.

14. *New York Times*, December 9, 1937.

15. Galíndez, *Era of Trujillo*, 37

16. Reynolds, "Murder in the Tropics," 36.

17. Reynolds, "Murder in the Tropics," 36.

18. Reynolds, "Murder in the Tropics," 36.

19. Reynolds, "Murder in the Tropics," 36.

20. Galíndez, *Era of Trujillo*, 38.

21. Galíndez, *Era of Trujillo*, 38.

22. Galíndez, *Era of Trujillo*, 39.

23. Crassweller, *Trujillo*, 134.

24. Crassweller, *Trujillo*, 135.

25. Crassweller, *Trujillo*, 135.

26. Ornes, *Trujillo*, 215.

27. Ornes, *Trujillo*, 298.

28. *New York Post*, July 1956, quoted in Ornes, *Trujillo*, 298.

29. Ornes, *Trujillo*, 313.

30. Diederich, *Trujillo*, 35.

31. Diederich, *Trujillo*, 4.

32. Crassweller, *Trujillo*, 85.

33. Ornes, *Trujillo*, 84.

34. Behnken and Wendt, *Crossing Boundaries*, 43.

35. *New York Times*, December 21, 1962.

36. *New York Times*, February 28, 1962.

37. Moya Pons, *Dominican Republic*, 385.

38. President Lyndon Johnson, "Report on the Situation in the Dominican Republic," May 2, 1965, http://loveman.sdsu.edu/docs/1965JohnsonDoctrine.pdf.

39. Moya Pons, *Dominican Republic*, 388.

40. Moya Pons, *Dominican Republic*, 390

41. Moya Pons, *Dominican Republic*, 390

42. Moya Pons, *Dominican Republic*, 390

43. Read Vittini, *Trujillo de cerca*, 13.

44. Gerón, *Diccionario político dominicano*, 449.

45. *New York Times*, February 15, 1997.

46. *Siglo*, March 5, 1997.

19. The Persevering Paige

1. *Pittsburgh Courier*, May 1, 1937.

2. *Chicago Daily Tribune*, June 17, 1937, bracketed text in original.

3. *Chicago Defender*, July 10, 1937.

4. *Listín Diario*, July 7, 1937.

5. *Chicago Defender*, August 21, 1937.

6. *Lincoln Evening Journal*, August 12, 1937.

7. *Chicago Defender*, August 21, 1937.

8. *Pittsburgh Courier*, October 2, 1937.

9. *Chicago Defender*, September 25, 1937.

10. *Afro-American*, October 16, 1937.

11. *Afro-American*, October 16, 1937.

12. Quoted in *Afro-American*, October 16, 1937.
13. Tygiel, *Baseball's Great Experiment*, 30.
14. *Los Angeles News*, cited in *Chicago Defender*, August 15, 1942.
15. Paige, *Maybe I'll Pitch Forever*, 121.
16. Paige, *Maybe I'll Pitch Forever*, 121.
17. *Afro-American*, February 5, 1938.
18. *Afro-American*, February 26, 1938.
19. *Pittsburgh Courier*, April 16, 1938.
20. *Pittsburgh Courier*, April 23, 1938.
21. *Afro-American*, May 21, 1938.
22. *Pittsburgh Courier*, October 29, 1938.
23. Paige, *Maybe I'll Pitch Forever*, 86.
24. Paige, *Maybe I'll Pitch Forever*, 123.
25. Santana Alonso, *El Inmortal de béisbol*, 78–82.
26. Santana Alonso, *El Inmortal de béisbol*, 78–82.
27. *El Nacional* (Mexico City), September 19, 1938.
28. Paige, *Maybe I'll Pitch Forever*, 129.
29. *Chicago Defender*, December 12, 1938.
30. Paige, *Maybe I'll Pitch Forever*, 122.
31. Paige, *Maybe I'll Pitch Forever*, 130.
32. Fox, *Satchel Paige's America*, 111.
33. Circle Records 1948, Jelly Roll Morton, cover notes by Rudi Blesh.
34. *Monroe (LA) Morning Herald*, May 7, 1939.
35. *Paris (TX) News*, May 21, 1939.
36. Paige, *Maybe I'll Pitch Forever*, 134.
37. *Iola (KS) Register*, May 31, 1938.
38. *Satchel Paige's America*, 113.
39. *Winnipeg Free Press*, June 20, 1939.
40. Fox, *Satchel Paige's America*, 113.
41. *Bismarck (ND) Tribune*, June 26, 1939.
42. *Billings (MT) Gazette*, June 27, 1939.
43. *Nevada State Journal*, July 30, 1939.
44. Fox, *Satchel Paige's America*, 115.
45. Fox, *Satchel Paige's America*, 115.
46. Young, *Great Negro Baseball Stars*, 24.
47. Rogosin, *Invisible Men*, 189.
48. Paige, *Maybe I'll Pitch Forever*, 181.
49. Paige, *Maybe I'll Pitch Forever*, 197.
50. Paige, *Maybe I'll Pitch Forever*, 197.
51. Paige, *Maybe I'll Pitch Forever*, 197.
52. Fox, *Satchel Paige's America*, 101.
53. Fox, *Satchel Paige's America*, 102.

54. Paige, *Pitchin' Man*, 10.
55. Paige, *Pitchin' Man*, 11.
56. Paige, *Maybe I'll Pitch Forever*, 203.
57. Ebony, *March* 1969.
58. Young, *Great Negro Baseball Stars*, 88.
59. Paige, *Maybe I'll Pitch Forever*, 223.
60. Veeck, *Veeck as in Wreck*, 190.
61. Veeck, *Veeck as in Wreck*, 191.
62. Fox, *Satchel Paige's America*, 14. Stengel was an admirer of Paige as witnessed by his naming him to the roster of the American League All-Star Team in both 1952 and 1953.
63. Fox, *Satchel Paige's America*, 93.

20. "El Gamo"

1. Center for Negro League Baseball Research, Negro League Baseball, Historical Timeline, http://www.cnlbr.org/Portals/0/RL/Historical%20Timeline.pdf.
2. Cordova, *Tetelo Vargas "El Gamo,"* 21.
3. Cordova, *Tetelo Vargas "El Gamo,"* 15.
4. *Afro-American*, August 1, 1931; Cordova, *Tetelo Vargas "El Gamo,"* 20.
5. Cordova, *Tetelo Vargas "El Gamo,"* 24.
6. Inoa and Cruz, *Baseball in Dominican Republic*, 111.
7. Crassweller, *Trujillo*, 184.
8. Cordova, *Tetelo Vargas "El Gamo,"* 28.
9. Cordova, *Tetelo Vargas "El Gamo,"* 41.
10. Cordova, *Tetelo Vargas "El Gamo,"* 42.
11. Cordova, *Tetelo Vargas "El Gamo,"* 51.

21. Y Otras

1. Holway, *Voices*, 128–29. Sitting out the final game meant that Cool Papa would have too few at bats to qualify for the batting title; this ensured that Irvin would win.
2. McCormack, *Cool Papa Bell*, 85.
3. McCormack, *Cool Papa Bell*, 87.
4. Revel and Munoz, *Pedro Anibal "Perucho" Cepeda*, 3–4.
5. Van Hyning, *Puerto Rico's Winter League*, 73.
6. Van Hyning, *Puerto Rico's Winter League*, 74.
7. Revel and Munoz, *Pedro Anibal "Perucho" Cepeda*, 5.
8. *Listín Diario*, April 19, 1937.
9. *Listín Diario*, May 3, 1937.
10. *Listín Diario*, May 10, 1937.
11. *Listín Diario*, May 17, 1937.
12. *Listín Diario*, July 1, 1937.

13. Cordova, *Tetelo Vargas "El Gamo,"* 26.

14. Rory Costello, SABR Baseball Biography Project, Luis E. Tiant, http://sabr .org/bioproj/person/af5fffe8.

15. Mark Armour, SABR Baseball Biography Project, Luis E. Tiant, http://sabr .org/bioproj/person/2212deaf.

16. *Oregonian*, September 6, 2010.

17. *New York Times*, October 3, 1972.

18. *New York Times*, May 9, 1975.

19. *New York Times*, August 27, 1975.

20. *New York Times*, August 27, 1975.

21. *New York Times*, December 15, 1976.

22. *New York Times*, December 17, 1976.

Appendix

1. *Los Angeles Times*, January 21, 1935.

2. *San Diego Sun*, February 21, 1935.

3. Patterson and Gowdy, *Golden Voices of Baseball*, 74.

4. Introduction to 1993 edition of Paige's *Maybe I'll Pitch Forever* (University of Nebraska Press).

5. *San Diego Sun*, February 23, 1935.

6. *The San Diego Union*, February 23, 1935. The two newspapers disagree about the number of batters Paige struck out. The *Sun* put the number at seventeen and the *Union* at fifteen.

7. Williams, *Science of Hitting*, 58.

8. Williams, *Science of Hitting*, 58.

9. *Chattanooga Times*, May 2, 1926.

10. Motley, *Ruling over Monarchs*, 84.

11. Van Hyning, *Puerto Rico's Winter League*, 74.

12. *Listín Diario*, April 22, 1937.

13. Fox, *Satchel Paige's America*, 85.

14. The math on this point is simple: the mound is sixty feet, six inches from home plate. If a pitcher uses a long stride and a late release point, he can shave up to three feet (over normal stride and release point) extra off this distance. This accounts for a nearly 5 percent difference. If a pitcher throws a pitch at 90 miles per hour (132 feet per second) and it leaves his hand at fifty-seven feet, it will take .43 seconds to reach home plate. In contrast a pitch released at 54 feet will reach the plate in .41 seconds.

15. Donovan, "Fabulous Satchel Paige," 66–68.

16. Williams, *Science of Hitting*, 58.

17. Donovan, "Fabulous Satchel Paige," 65–66.

18. Donovan, "Fabulous Satchel Paige," 69.

19. Trouppe, *20 Years Too Soon*, 55.

20. Lewis, *It Takes All Kinds*, 181.
21. Lewis, *It Takes All Kinds*, 181.
22. Mays, *Say Hey*, 27–28.
23. Lewis, *It Takes All Kinds*, 182.
24. Paige, *Pitchin' Man*, 68.
25. Paige, *Pitchin' Man*, 67.
26. Donovan, "Fabulous Satchel Paige," 69.
27. Donovan, "Fabulous Satchel Paige," 69.
28. Paige, *Pitchin' Man*, 76.
29. Lewis, *It Takes All Kinds*, 182.
30. Williams, *Science of Hitting*, 58.
31. *Colliers*, June 6, 1953, 22.
32. Paige, *Pitchin' Man*, 31.
33. Donovan, "Fabulous Satchel Paige," 69.
34. Paige, *Pitchin' Man*, 11, 67.
35. Paige, *Pitchin' Man*, 68–69.
36. Lewis, *It Takes All Kinds*, 179.
37. Trouppe, *20 Years Too Soon*, 55.
38. Lewis, *It Takes All Kinds*, 179.
39. Lewis, *It Takes All Kinds*, 180.

BIBLIOGRAPHY

Ariza, Sander. *Trujillo: The Man and His Country.* New York: Orlin Tremaine, 1939.

Bankes, James. *The Pittsburgh Crawfords: The Lives and Times of Black Baseball's Most Exciting Team.* Dubuque IA: Wm. C. Brown, 1991.

Barthel, Thomas. *Baseball Barnstorming and Exhibition Games, 1901–1962: A History of Off-Season Major League Play.* Jefferson NC: McFarland, 2003.

Beals, Carlton. *America South.* London: J. B. Lippincott, 1937.

Behnken, Brian D., and Simon Wendt, eds. *Crossing Boundaries: Ethnicity, Race, and National Belonging in a Transnational World.* Lanham MD: Lexington Books, 2013.

Besault, Lawrence de. *President Trujillo: His Work and the Dominican Republic.* Washington DC: Washington Publishing, 1936.

Bjarkman, Peter C. "Baseball with a Latin Beat." Jefferson NC: McFarland, 1994.

———. *Martín Dihigo: Baseball's Least-Known Hall of Famer. Elysian Fields Quarterly* 18, no. 2 (1994): 22–39.

Blanco Fombona, Horacio. *El Tirano Ulises Heureaux.* Ciudad Trujillo: Editora Montalvo, 1943.

Bosch, Juan. *Causas de una tiranía sin ejemplo.* Santo Domingo: Alfa & Omega, 2007.

Brashler, William. *Josh Gibson: A Life in the Negro Leagues.* Chicago: Ivan R. Dee, 1978.

Brown, Wenzell. *Angry Men—Laughing Men: The Caribbean Caldron.* New York: Greenberg, 1947.

Bruce, Janet. *The Kansas City Monarchs: Champions of Black Baseball.* Lawrence: University Press of Kansas, 1985.

Calder, Bruce J. *The Impact of Intervention: The Dominican Republic during the U.S. Occupation of 1916–1924.* Princeton NJ: Markus Wiener, 2006.

Cooper, Page. *Sambumbia: A Discovery of the Dominican Republic, the Modern Hispaniola.* New York: Caribbean Library, 1947.

Cordova, Cuqui. *El campeonato de 1937.* Historia del béisbol dominicano 7. Santo Domingo: Impreso en Omnimedia, 2009.

———. *Horacio Martínez: El Rabbit.* Historia del béisbol dominicano 3. Santo Domingo: Impreso en Omnimedia, 2004.

————. *Los Hermanos Báez "Los Tres Grillos (A, B y C)."* Historia del béisbol dominicano 12. Santo Domingo: Impreso en Omnimedia, 2015.

————. *Tetelo Vargas "El Gamo."* Historia del béisbol dominicano 2. Santo Domingo: Impreso en Omnimedia, 2003.

Crassweller, Robert D. *Trujillo: The Life and Times of a Caribbean Dictator*. New York: Macmillan, 1966.

Derby, Lauren H. "The Dictators Seduction: Gender and State Spectacle During the Trujillo Regime." In *Latin American Popular Culture: An Introduction*, edited by William H. Beezley and Linda A. Curcio-Nagy, 213–39. Wilmington DE: Scholarly Resources, 2000.

Diederich, Bernard. *Trujillo: The Death of the Goat*. London: Bodley Head, 1978.

Donovan, Richard. "The Fabulous Satchel Paige." *Collier's Magazine*, May 30, 1953, 62–69.

Espaillat, Arturo R. *Trujillo: The Last Caesar*. Chicago: Henry Regnery, 1963.

Farson, Negley. *Transgressor in the Tropics*. Rahway NJ: Quinn & Boden, 1938.

Fox, William Price. *Satchel Paige's America*. Tuscaloosa: University of Alabama Press, 2005.

Frank, Harry A. *Roaming through the West Indies*. New York: Grossett & Dunlap, 1920.

Fuller, Stephen M., and Graham A. Cosmas. *Marines in the Dominican Republic 1916–1924*. Washington DC: History and Museums Division, U.S. Marine Corps, 1974.

Gardner, Robert, and Dennis Shortelle. *The Forgotten Players: The Story of Black Baseball in America*. New York: Walker, 1993.

Gerón, Cándido. *Diccionario político dominicano: 1821–2000*. Santo Domingo: Editora de Colores, 1993.

Galíndez, Jesús de. *The Era of Trujillo, Dominican Dictator*. Tucson: University of Arizona Press, 1973.

González Echevarria, Roberto. *The Pride of Havana: A History of Cuban Baseball*. New York: Oxford University Press, 2001.

Gunther, John. *Inside Latin America*. New York: Harper & Brothers, 1940.

Hart, Hastings H. *Social Progress of Alabama: A Second Study of the Social Institutions and Agencies of the State of Alabama*. New York: Russell Sage Foundation, 1918.

Hazard, Samuel. *Santo Domingo, Past and Present: With a Glance at Hayti*. New York: Harper & Bros., 1873.

Hicks, Albert C. *Blood in the Streets*. New York: Creative Age Press, 1924.

Holway, John. *Black Diamonds: Life in the Negro Leagues from the Men Who Lived It*. Westport CT: Meckler, 1989.

————. *Blackball Stars: Negro League Pioneers*. New York: Carroll & Graf, 1992.

————. *Josh and Satch: The Life and Times of Josh Gibson and Satchel Paige*. Westport CT: Meckler, 1991.

————. *Voices from the Great Black Baseball Leagues*. Dodd, Mead, 1975.

Infante, Fernando. *Biografía de Trujillo*. Santo Domingo: Editorial Letra Graphica, 2009.

Ingham, John N., and Lynne B. Feldman. *African-American Business Leaders: A Biographical Dictionary*. Westport CT: Greenwood Press, 1993.

Inman, Samuel Guy. *Through Santo Domingo and Haiti: A Cruise with the Marines*. New York: Committee on Co-operation in Latin America, 1919.

———. *Trailing the Conquistadores*. New York: Friendship Press, 1930.

Inoa, Orlando, and Héctor J. Cruz. *Baseball in Dominican Republic: Chronicle of a Passion*. Santo Domingo: Verizon Cultural Collection, 2005.

Jáquez, José. *Sin miedo a Trujillo*. Santo Domingo: Editorial Argos, 2011.

Jones, Chester Lloyd. *The Caribbean since 1900*. New York: Prentice-Hall, 1936.

Jones, Thomas Jesse. *Negro Education: A Study of the Private and Higher Schools for Colored People in the United States*. Washington DC: U.S. Office of Education, Phelps-Stokes Fund, U.S. Government Printing Office, 1917.

Kirkpatrick, F. A. *Latin America: A Brief History*. New York: Macmillan, 1939.

Klein, Alan M. *Sugarball: The American Game, the Dominican Dream*. New Haven CT: Yale University Press, 1991.

Knight, Melvin M. *The Americans in Santo Domingo*. New York: Vanguard Press, 1928.

———. *Los Americanos en Santo Domingo: Estudios de Imperialismo Americano*. Ciudad Trujillo: Publicaciones de la Universidad de Santo Domingo, Listín Diario, 1939.

Krich, John. *El Béisbol: Travels through the Pan-American Pastime*. New York: Atlantic Monthly Press, 1989.

Lamb, Chris. *Conspiracy of Silence: Sportswriters and the Long Campaign to Desegregate Baseball*. Lincoln: University of Nebraska Press, 2012.

Lanctot, Neil. *Negro League Baseball: The Rise and Ruin of a Black Institution*. Philadelphia: University of Pennsylvania Press, 2004.

Langley, Lester D. *The United States and the Caribbean, 1900–1970*. Athens: University of Georgia Press, 1980.

Lewis, Lloyd. *It Takes All Kinds*. New York: Harcourt, Brace, 1947.

Mays, Willie. *Say Hey: The Autobiography of Willie Mays*. With Lou Sahadi. New York: Simon & Schuster, 1988.

McCormack, Shaun. *Cool Papa Bell*. New York: Rosen, 2002.

McNeil, William F. *Baseball's Other All-Stars*. Jefferson NC: McFarland, 2000.

———. *Cool Papas and Double Duties*. Jefferson NC: McFarland, 2001.

Medina Benet, Victor M. *Fracaso de la Tercera Republica: Los responsables; Narraciones de historia dominicana, 1924–1930*. N.p.: Sociedad Dominicana de Bibliófilos, 2013.

Mejia, Luis F. *De Lilís a Trujillo: Historia contemporánea de la República Dominicana*. Santo Domingo: Editoria de Santo Domingo, 1976.

Motley, Bob. *Ruling over Monarchs, Giants & Stars: Umpiring in the Negro Leagues & Beyond*. Champaign IL: Sports Publishing, 2007.

Moya Pons, Frank. *The Dominican Republic: A National History*. Princeton NJ: Markus Wiener, 1998.

———. *History of the Caribbean*. Princeton NJ: Markus Wiener, 2007.

Murphy, Martin F. *Dominican Sugar Plantations*. New York: Praeger, 1991.

Nanita, Abelardo R. *Trujillo: The Biography of a Great Leader*. New York: Vantage Press, 1957.

Newman, Oliver P. "The Land Columbus Loved." *National Geographic*, February 1944, 196–224.

Ornes, Germain E. *Trujillo: Little Caesar of the Caribbean*. New York: Thomas Nelson & Sons, 1958.

Paige, Satchel. *Maybe I'll Pitch Forever*. Garden City NY: Doubleday, 1962.

———. "My Biggest Baseball Day." *Negro Digest*, May 1943, 7–10.

———. *Pitchin' Man*. As told to Hal Lebovitz. Cleveland: Self-published, 1948.

Papers relating to the Foreign Relations of the United States. Washington DC: U.S. Government Printing Office, 1909.

Patterson, Ted, and Curt Gowdy. *The Golden Voices of Baseball*. Champaign IL: Sports Publishing, 2002.

Peterson, Robert. *Only the Ball Was White*. New York: McGraw-Hill, 1970.

Read Vittini, Mario. *Trujillo de cerca*. Santo Domingo: Editora San Rafael 2007.

Reisler, Jim. *Black Writers/Black Baseball*. Jefferson NC: McFarland, 2007.

Revel, Layton, and Luis Munoz. *Pedro Anibal "Perucho" Cepeda*. Forgotten Heroes. Carrollton TX: Center for Negro League Baseball Research, 2009.

Reynolds, Quentin. "Murder in the Tropics." *Colliers*, January 22, 1938, 14–15, 34–36.

Ribowsky, Mark. *Don't Look Back: Satchel Paige in the Shadows of Baseball*. New York: Simon & Schuster, 1994.

———. *The Power and the Darkness: The Life of Josh Gibson in the Shadows of the Game*. Urbana: University of Illinois Press, 1994.

Riley, James A. *The Biographical Encyclopedia of the Negro Leagues*. New York: Carroll & Graf, 1994.

Rodman, Selden. *Quisqueya: A History of the Dominican Republic*. Seattle: University of Washington Press, 1964.

Rogosin, Donn. *Invisible Men: Life in Baseball's Negro Leagues*. Lincoln: University of Nebraska Press, 2007.

Roorda, Eric. *The Dictator Next Door: The Good Neighbor Policy and the Trujillo Regime in the Dominican Republic, 1930–1945*. Durham NC: Duke University Press, 1998.

Ruck, Rob. *The Tropic of Baseball: Baseball in the Dominican Republic*. Westport CT: Meckler, 1991.

Rueda, Manuel. *Bienvenida y la noche: Crónicas de Montecristi*. Santo Domingo: Fundación Cultural Dominicana, 1994.

Santana Alonso, Alfredo L. *El inmortal del béisbol Martín Dihigo*. La Habana, Cuba: Editorial Cientifico-Técnica, 2007.

Schoenrich, Otto. *Santo Domingo: A Country with a Future*. New York: Macmillan, 1918.

Thomason, Michael V. R. *Mobile: The New History of Alabama's First City*. Tuscaloosa: University of Alabama Press, 2001.

Treto Cisneros, Pedro. *The Mexican League: Comprehensive Player Statistics, 1973–2001/La Liga Mexicana: Estadísticas comprensivas de los jugadores, 1937–2001*. Jefferson NC: McFarland, 2002.

Trouppe, Quincy. *20 Years Too Soon: Prelude to Major-League Integrated Baseball*. St. Louis: Missouri Historical Society Press, 1995.

Turkin, Hy. *The Official Encyclopedia of Baseball*. New York: A. S. Barnes, 1956.

Tye, Larry. *Satchel: The Life and Time of an American Legend*. New York: Random House, 2009.

Tygiel, Jules. *Baseball's Great Experiment: Jackie Robinson and His Legacy*. New York: Oxford University Press, 1983.

Vandercook, John W. *Caribee Cruise: A Book of the West Indies*. New York: Reynal & Hitchcock, 1938.

Van Hyning, Thomas E. *Puerto Rico's Winter League: A History of Major League Baseball's Launching Pad*. Foreword by Eduardo Valero. Jefferson NC: McFarland, 2004.

Vargas Llosa, Mario. *The Feast of the Goat*. New York: Picador, 2001.

Veeck, William Louis, Jr. *Veeck as in Wreck: The Autobiography of Bill Veeck*. With Edward Linn. Chicago: University of Chicago Press, 2001.

Vega, Bernardo. *Cien años del Listín*. Santo Domingo: Listín Diario, 1996.

Vega y Pagan, Ernesto. *Military Biography of Generalissimo Rafael Trujillo Molina, Commander in Chief of the Armed Forces*. Ciudad Trujillo: Editorial Atenas, 1956.

Verrill, Hyatt. *The Book of the West Indies*. New York: E. P. Dutton, 1919.

Walker, Stanley. *Journey toward the Sunlight*. New York: Caribbean Library, 1947.

Welles, Sumner. *Naboth's Vineyard: The Dominican Republic, 1844–1924*. 2 vols. Mamaroneck NY: Paul P. Appel, 1966.

White, Sol. *Sol White's History of Colored Base Ball*. Lincoln: University of Nebraska Press, 1995.

Williams, Ted. *The Science of Hitting*. New York: Simon & Schuster, 1986.

Williams, Ted, and John Underwood. *My Turn at Bat: The Story of My Life*. New York: Simon & Schuster, 1969.

Young, A. S. "Doc." *Great Negro Baseball Stars and How They Made the Major Leagues*. New York: A. S. Barnes, 1953.

INDEX